JULIO CORTÁZAR

A Study of the Short Fiction

Twayne's Studies in Short Fiction

Gordon Weaver, General Editor
Oklahoma State University

Julio Cortázar. *Photograph by Layle Silbert. Reproduced by permission.*

JULIO CORTÁZAR

A Study of the Short Fiction

Ilan Stavans
Amherst College

TWAYNE PUBLISHERS
An Imprint of Simon & Schuster Macmillan
New York

PRENTICE HALL INTERNATIONAL
London   Mexico City   New Delhi   Singapore   Sydney   Toronto

Twayne's Studies in Short Fiction, No. 63

Twayne Publishers
An Imprint of Simon & Schuster Macmillan
1633 Broadway
New York, NY 10019

Library of Congress Cataloging-in-Publication Data

Stavans, Ilan.
    Julio Cortázar : a study of the short fiction / Ilan Stavans.
        p.   cm.—(Twayne's studies in short fiction ; no. 63)
    Includes bibliographical references and index.
    ISBN 0-8057-8293-1 (cloth)
    1. Cortázar, Julio—Criticism and interpretation.   2. Short story.   I.
Title.   II. Series.
    PQ7797.C7145Z795   1996
    863—dc20
                                                                                            95-32554
                                                                                            CIP

The paper used in this publication meets the minimum requirements of American National Standard for Information Sciences—Permanence of Paper for Printed Library Materials, ANSI Z39.48–1984. ⊚ ™

10 9 8 7 6 5 4 3 2 1

Printed in the United States of America

For Daniel Nahson

The aspects of things that are most important to us are hidden because of their simplicity and familiarity.

Ludwig Wittgenstein, *Philosophical Investigations*

Contents

Preface

"Anybody who doesn't read Julio Cortázar is doomed," the Chilean poet and diplomat Pablo Neruda once said and, at least on this particular issue, he wasn't off target. A master of two genres—the novel and short story—the Argentine (1914–84) was very much in vogue in the 1960s and 1970s in Europe, the United States, and Latin America, and his 1963 masterpiece, *Hopscotch*, alongside Gabriel García Márquez's *One Hundred Years of Solitude* (1967), is considered today a cornerstone of Hispanic fiction in particular and world letters in general.

But since his death more than a decade ago, Cortázar has mysteriously fallen out of public favor. Seldom read beyond college courses, his style and voice are seen as the legacy of an era long gone and buried, one that took jazz out of the nightclub and into the concert hall. He was obsessively involved in experimenting with drugs to reach alternative levels of consciousness. If to read Cortázar at the peak of his international reputation was to submerge oneself in the art of improvisational, empirical narrative, to open one of his books today is to return to an age when the writer wasn't a mere entertainer and superstar but, instead, helped to open alternative cognitive windows, when fiction was considered by many as useful a tool in the understanding of history and philosophy as any scientific discipline. An unconventional man of letters and an intellectual explorer, Cortázar was born in Brussels and exiled in Europe since 1951, but he was an Argentine from head to toe. He would trot the globe denouncing human-rights violations and would spend hours in front of the typewriter professing to own a unique method of writing short stories not unlike those developed by the French surrealist André Breton and the American Beat writer Jack Kerouac. A story, Cortázar claimed, is born in a sparkle, a thunderous strike of inspiration, and requires very little by way of processing. He perfected the technique known as "automatic writing," in which the writer, much like Samuel Taylor Coleridge when drafting *Kubla Khan* (1797) after an opium-induced dream, must learn to trust his gut feelings. Almost no rewritings and virtually no additional editing are needed once the text appears on the page; it is as if literature were only the product of a spirit dictating his craft to numerous scribes everywhere on the globe. He wrote a handful of tales that, to my mind, are among the best this century has delivered, including "Axolotl," about a man trapped in the body of a salamander; "House Taken Over," about the effects of tyranny on individual freedom and domestic life; and "Blow-Up," about the moral implications that emerge after one witnesses a crime.

Novels, on the other hand, were for Cortázar the result of accumulation and a cut-and-paste development. His story lines were always restricted to the bizarre and unexplained, even when a political message was intermingled. Although his fantastic tales deal with the double, the labyrinth, and transformations of humans into beasts—themes typical of two major influential writers on his work, Edgar Allan Poe and Jorge Luis Borges—he infused his stories with a dreamlike, surrealistic cadence. He would describe Anton Chekhov's style as a storyteller as directed toward explaining, in minute detail, a man's routine while his own approach to literature, following the rhythm of chance, was interested in exceptions to a rule—not the investigation of senseless repetitions of an act but the sudden abolition of a habit.

Reading is thinking with the mind of a stranger. I can vividly recall first reading Julio Cortázar, back in 1978, as a 17-year-old aspiring writer. I bought *Hopscotch* in Librería Gandhi, in Coyoacán, a southern suburb in Mexico City. A few months before a close friend had given me a recording the Argentine had done of his early short story "House Taken Over," as part of a series produced by Radio Universidad Nacional Autónoma de México. On the album cover Cortázar appeared tall, charming, and rather young, even childish for his 54 years. His voice was deep, and his Spanish was awkward, as if spoken by a foreigner; his guttural French "r" was an unmistakable trademark many could never forget. Pablo Neruda, for instance, constantly referred to Cortázar's "r" when talking about the Argentine in interviews and conversations. To me, "House Taken Over," a tale about incestuous siblings inhabiting a ghost-invaded building, was tantalizing. Echoes of H. P. Lovecraft (whom, I later discovered, Cortázar hated) and Poe's "The Fall of the House of Usher" could be heard everywhere. But Cortázar was not a derivative writer: he had his own voice.[1]

Around the time I bought *Hopscotch* I was planning a trip to California and Texas and was considering taking with me a few "necessary titles" from the so-called Latin American Boom, a literary movement of the late 1960s and 1970s. Aside from Cortázar, I remember taking with me Carlos Fuentes's *A Change of Skin* and Mario Vargas Llosa's *The Green House*. Although the three were essentially different but complemented one another, *Hopscotch* was, unlike the other two, a masterpiece. Fuentes, who's probably more admired today for the ambition he pours into his works than for the works themselves, was concerned with history and mass media in his book, but the prose seemed to me repetitive, even boring. I couldn't find a single memorable moment in a Fuentes novel, one dazzling beautiful description, a character really alive, one reminding us of people we have met or would like to have known. Vargas Llosa, on the other hand, was an enchanting realist in the tradition of Flaubert and Dos Passos, but his prose didn't have the experimental edge I was looking for. In my eyes, Cortázar was simply outstanding. I admired his joi de vivre, his innovative, avant-garde, authentic voice, his passion to dare, to bring to test, to turn the universe upside down, to play around with trivia, to have a dry turn. Since that trip I have reread *Hopscotch* at least a half dozen times. As I jumped from chapter to chapter, I knew I was undergoing a rite of passage. The style was at once vivid and atypical. The themes—exile, the divided self—dealt with an important facet of modern life: nostalgia for the place called home, a desire to return to the womb.

Cortázar's linguistic odyssey also attracted me. When, in 1985, I left Mexico to settle in the United States, I made the conscious decision to master English. My hope, impossible though it might seem, was to live in two worlds, to become a bridge between the cultures divided by the Rio Grande. At first my Spanish suffered tremendously. Editors in my native country would send letters of complaint arguing that I was writing in Spanish but thinking in English. While investigating the complexities of my polyglotism, I have often returned to *Hopscotch*, which was written in Europe, and cannot but feel a sense of wonder at Cortázar's language. His isn't a pure idiom but a *ménage*, an intoxication, a hybrid, an invention: half-Cervantes, half-Rabelais, seasoned with a twist of John Barth. If anything, Cortázar's Spanish—or shall I say *SFpraennicshh?*—is an extraordinary display of the hardships of a transitory existence in a world where mass migrations, culture collisions, and easy jet travel are ubiquitous. Cortázar's linguistic experiment is one of his most remarkable contributions: he reinvented the Spanish language, made it more malleable, a docile tongue ready to incorporate the angst of modern existence.

Some fifteen years after my first discovery of Cortázar, my opinion

Preface

of him has somewhat changed, his aura of genius having receded. While in my mind *Hopscotch* is still astonishing, other of Cortázar's novels, from *The Winners* on, I have found trite and unappealing, certainly not his best work. I identify with the narrator of "We Love Glenda So Much," a remarkable story published in 1980: I am tempted to change segments, reverse structures, and improve wasted endings. The lyricism and power of these novels sooner or later ends up demolished by a lack of focus and a dispensable structure. A handful of his stories, on the other hand, beginning with "Instructions for John Howell," "The Other Heaven" (a tribute to Lautréamont's *Chants de Maldoror*), and "Blow-Up," are remarkable achievements. Half a dozen are simply extraordinary, and some 20 are memorable. Thus, I have switched my allegiance from Cortázar the amorphous novelist to Cortázar the subversive storyteller. Whereas such critics as Uruguayan Emir Rodríguez Monegal believe Cortázar was at his best in the novel, I believe that the field of short fiction is where he might have done his best work.

This volume is devoted solely to Cortázar's short fiction. My objective here is to do what critics today find quite prohibitive: to use his art to enlighten his life, and vice versa. While at times I refer to his craft as novelist and translator, I have tried to limit my analysis to the ways in which, by choosing to rebuff, imitate, or pay homage to Borges, Poe, Felisberto Hernández, Horacio Quiroga, and Roberto Arlt, as well as Chekov, Lautréamont, and other writers, he found his own unique style. Because Cortázar's existential journey from Brussels to Buenos Aires to Paris and the small town of Saignon in southern France is never studied vis-á-vis his oeuvre, I have chosen a decisively confessional approach: mine is an *autobiography* of his short fiction, an overall analysis of his talents in the genre as they developed throughout his life—life as art and art as life. While Cortázar often refused to discuss personal matters with interviewers, and, what's truly baffling, more than a decade after his death there is still no full-length biography of him available, here and there he offered enough information for astute readers, in a cut-and-paste approach, to build a comprehensive view of his journey. My goal is to use this information as background, to understand where the 100 or so stories he wrote came from and what they mean in the overall landscape of his personal and creative journey.

Although I devote the bulk of this text to analyzing, in more or less chronological sequence, selected tales, most of which are part of four collections available in English—*End of the Game* (1963), *A Change*

Preface

of Light (1970), *All Fires the Fire* (1980), and *We Love Glenda So Much* (1983)—I try to see them in biographical context. Those interested in a thematic division of his short fiction should consult the works of critics like Jaime Alazraki and Rosario Ferré, whose comments I discuss in the text. More than anything else, mine is the praise of one Latin American writer for his precursor, the personal testimony of a passion for Cortázar's originality, which greatly influenced my own way of thinking and writing. The analysis of Cortázar I present here is an affidavit of my own perspective—it is subjective and perhaps even capricious.

Part 1 is divided into 10 subparts; its subtitles pick up on a certain motif of that segment, although that motif will certainly reappear elsewhere in the volume. The section begins by studying Cortázar's artistic development from the early 1940s until 1951; it then analyzes what he wrote in Paris (i.e., away from the place once called home, Buenos Aires) and continues by tracing his favorite themes and symbols, paying special attention to his long story, or novella, "The Pursuer," considered by many a transitional work. Finally, it analyzes Cortázar's ideological commitment during the student uprising in Paris in 1968, his views on the Cuban Revolution and the Sandinistas in Nicaragua, and the so-called ideological stories he wrote. Although Cortázar published fantastic and political tales from the outset until shortly before his death, I suggest two more-or-less clearly defined creative periods: 1945–66 and 1967–83; that is, until *All Fires the Fire* and after. This division is justified because during the next epoch he advocated a literature distant from earthly affairs, while in the second he supported artistic freedom and, simultaneously, invited writers to be active, both physically and intellectually, in the revolutionary transformation he hoped would change the face of Latin America for ever once the Fidel Castro regime in Havana established itself as a role model. Hence, the author of "Axolotl" and other masterful tales ought to be seen as a transitional figure in the literary landscape from south of the Rio Grande—from ivory tower to urban guerrilla, a vivid example of a culturally sophisticated artist who travels from isolation to militant fervor, a naive romantic dreaming of a utopian future in the wasteland.

In order to interpret various possible readings emerging from a single text, I often bring forth the view of various critics, such as Evelyn Picon Garfield, Terry J. Peavler, and Luis Harss. In Part 2 I have gathered what to my mind is Cortázar's best explanation of what makes a short story unique and what its uses are: "On the Short Story and

xv

Its Environs," part of *Around the Day in Eighty Worlds,* a substantial selection of which text was reprinted in the *New York Times Book Review.* It is accompanied by a couple of insightful personal essays, "The Present State of Fiction in Latin America" and "Letter to Roberto Fernández Retamar," which clarifies Cortázar's method of writing, his esthetic approach to the natural and supernatural (*lo real* and *lo fantástico*), and maps his view on the role artists and intellectuals are called to play in the so-called Third World. When read together, these entries offer a complete, sharp self-portrait of the writer's two creative periods. As counterpoint, Part 3 offers a comprehensive view of Cortázar's art as a writer in general and as a practitioner of short fiction in particular: John Ditski studies the Argentine's early works, while Evelyn Pico Garfield, a longtime Cortázar devotee and the author of an insightful book-long interview with him, focuses on *Octaedro* (1974).

All titles in this volume are translated into English, followed by the Spanish original; when a text is not available in translation, I say so. The Chronology offers a concise sequence of Cortázar's life and work, the most complete and up-to-date I know. The Bibliography lists everything Cortázar wrote in Spanish known today, be it fiction, nonfiction, poetry, drama, and translations. It also includes every translated story and novel of his into English, as well as special issues of U.S. and Latin American journals devoted to his oeuvre, important interviews, and essential critical works dealing with his art, particularly his short fiction. The translations I used throughout the volume are those universally available, unless I was forced to translate myself because of the unavailability of a certain story in English.

In one of his rare interviews, published in 1984, the year he died, Cortázar lamented that

> When all is said and done . . . I feel very much alone, and I think that's as it should be. In other words, I don't rely on Western tradition alone as a valid passport, and culturally I'm also totally disconnected from Eastern tradition, which I don't see any particular compensatory reason to lean on either. The truth is, each day I lose more confidence in myself, and I'm happy. I write worse and worse, from an esthetic point of view. I'm glad, because I think I'm approaching the point where perhaps I'll be able to start writing as I think one ought to write in our time. It may seem a kind of suicide, in a sense, but it's better to be a suicide than a zombie. It may be absurd for a writer to insist on discarding his work instruments. But I think those instruments are false. I want to wipe my slate clean, start from scratch.[2]

Cortázar dared to subvert literary dogmas. He understood writing as a never-ending quest and as a childish game. The moment he finished a short story he was ready to start all over again—from scratch. He was essentially dissatisfied with language and literature and, simultaneously, had an incomparable talent to dare to travel to unknown artistic spheres. Throughout his short stories the reader is pushed to the limits of understanding and knowledge. That's why his stories serve as the best tool not only to map his creative talents but also to capture an era in modern literature in which literature dared to explore the foundations of reality.

Notes

1. I would later write a tribute to his story, a fiction entitled "House Repossessed," *Massachusetts Review* 36, no. 2 (Summer 1995): 259–65; included in *The One-Handed Pianist and Other Stories* (Albuquerque: University of New Mexico Press, 1996).

2. Luis Harss and Barbara Dohmann, "Julio Cortázar; or, The Slap in the Face," in *Into the Mainstream: Conversations with Latin-American Writers* (New York: Harper & Row, 1967), 209.

Acknowledgments

Segments of this book first appeared as "Julio Cortázar, 'La puerta condenada,' y los fantasmas," *Plural* 17, no. 204 (1988): 86–90, and "Kafka, Cortázar, Gass," *Review of Contemporary Fiction* 11, no. 3 (Fall 1991): 131–36. © 1983 by the *Review of Contemporary Fiction*. I wish to thank my friend Steve Moore at Dalkey Archive Press for permission to reprint John Ditski's "*End of the Game:* The Early Fictions of Julio Cortázar," *Review of Contemporary Fiction* 3, no. 3 (Fall 1983): 38–44. Acknowledgment is also due to Thomas Christensen for permission to reprint Cortázar's "On the Short Story and Its Environs," translated by Mr. Christensen, from *Around the Day in Eighty Worlds* (San Francisco: North Point Press, 1986), 158–67. English translation © 1986 by Thomas Christensen. And to the Regents of the University of Oklahoma for permission to reprint Cortázar's "The Present State of Fiction in Latin America" and "*Octaedro:* Eight Phases of Despair," by Evelyn Picon Garfield, from *The Final Island: The Fiction of Julio Cortázar*, edited by Jaime Alazraki and Ivar Ivask (Norman: University of Oklahoma Press, 1976–78), 26–36 and 115–28, respectively. © 1976, 1978 by the University of Oklahoma Press. And to Jo Anne Engelbert for permission to reprint Cortázar's "Letter to Roberto Fernández Retamar," translated by Ms. Engelbert, from *Lives on the Line: The Testimony of Contemporary Latin American Authors*, edited by Doris Meyer (Los Angeles: University of California Press, 1988), 74–83.

Part 1

THE SHORT FICTION

In Borges's Wake

In the early 1980s Jorge Luis Borges, the celebrated Argentine man of letters responsible for "Emma Zunz," "The Secret Miracle," and other stories, embarked on an ambitious project. Hyspamérica, a publishing house in Buenos Aires, asked him to select more than 100 titles and write prologues to what would circulate as his own personal library. Before his death in Geneva in 1986, he managed to dictate 72 brief introductions to some of these volumes, mostly to his former student and later companion, María Kodama (he was blind since his fifties and could not write them himself). Suprisingly, the first volume of the project was an anthology of Julio Cortázar's stories. (Others included works by Oscar Wilde, Kafka, Jonathan Swift, H. G. Wells, and Rudyard Kipling). It was an unexpected move because in interviews and essays Borges had made it clear he could not take seriously enough the oeuvre of his compatriot. Their narrative techniques and political views, especially after December 1958, when the Cuban Revolution shook the Latin American intelligentsia, were in opposite extremes. One man was a meticulous craftsman, an enemy of the surrealist method of automatic writing, a passionate fan of Robert Louis Stevenson and *The Thousand and One Nights*, a right-wing librarian who at one time praised the dictatorial regime of General Augusto Pinochet in Chile. The other was a zealous and hot-tempered avant-gardist, a devotee of the early South American storytellers Felisberto Hernández and Horacio Quiroga. The former looked down on the latter as derivative, an author "who wrote bad the tales that Poe had already written well"— first an anarchist at heart, then a supporter of Fidel Castro and the 1979 Sandinista uprising in Nicaragua. One could even claim Borges was Cortázar's antithesis; the two men exhibited opposing viewpoints on almost everything, were political antagonists, and understood literature very differently indeed. One saw writing as a means to overcome oblivion and achieve immortality; the other believed in writing as a weapon to fight military repression and moral injustice. What, then, could suddenly draw Borges to praise Cortázar? Why such change of heart?

3

Part 1

The answer, I believe, points to a complex, intriguing, and labyrinthine relationship between the two Argentines—one marked by recognition of their individual talent and, in ideological terms, by mutual respect. "Around nineteen forty something," says Borges in his prologue to Cortázar's work, "I was managing editor of a more or less secret literary review. An afternoon like all others, a very tall young man, whose features I can't remember, brought me a short story in manuscript form. I told him he should return in 10 days to get my opinion. He came back a week later. I said I liked it and had already sent it to typesetting. Shortly after, Juilio Cortázar saw 'House Taken Over' ['Casa tomada'] printed alongside two pencil illustrations by [my sister, the artist] Nora Borges. Years passed by and a night in Paris, he confided me that it was his first text ever published. I'm honored to have been the instrument." He continues:

> The theme of the story is the gradual occupation of a house by an invisible presence. In future tales Julio Cortázar would return to the subject with a more indirect, and therefore efficient, approach. When Dante Gabriel Rossetti read the novel *Wuthering Heights*, he wrote to a friend: "The action takes place in hell, but the landscape, I don't know why, has English names." Something similar happens in Cortázar's oeuvre. His characters are deliberately trivial, ruled by a routine of casual affairs and battles. They even move around trivial things: cigarette brands, shopping windows, whisky, pharmacies, airports and train stations. They accept what is said in newspapers and the radio. Their topography is that of Buenos Aires or Paris and at first we might believe Corázar's stories are mere chronicles. But slowly we feel it isn't so. The narrator has brought us in a very subtle way to a terrible universe, one in which happiness is impossible—a broken universe where the lives of his characters are intermingled: the consciousness of a man can enter that of an animal and vice versa. Another device is to play with time—the substance with which we are made: in some tales two temporal stages cross over and are confused.
>
> The style is careless, but each word has been carefully selected. Nobody can recount one of Cortázar's plots; each text has a certain number of words and precise order. If we try to summarize it, something precious gets lost.[1]

The events described took place in 1946; "House Taken Over" ("Casa tomada"), one of Cortázar's most memorable pieces of short fiction, was published in *Los anales de Buenos Aires*. Five years later it became the opening entry in *Bestiary* (1951; *Bestiario*), Cortázar's first collection of stories, which appeared at a rather late age for a writer's debut, when he was pushing 40. To be sure, it was not the first time Cortázar would cross paths with the by-then already much respected author of *Labyrinths:* Borges would be his teacher some three years later, at the British Council in Buenos Aires, where he dictated a series of lectures on medieval British letters. As Cortázar repeatedly argued in interviews, he could not make it to every single session but attended one on Chaucer's *Canterbury Tales* that left him terribly impressed. "It was extraordinary," he would recall. So much so that "one of the memories I have of it, a sole sentence, became the title of a poem written in India in 1956 and a tribute to Borges, included in *Around the Day in Eighty Worlds* [*La vuelta al día en ochenta mundos*], 'The Smiler with the Knife Under the Cloak.' Uttered by a smiling character, Chaucer's phrase is the same line used by Argentine gauchos: *se viene con el cuchillo bajo el poncho.*"[2]

Ironically, for many people today, modern Argentine letters can be summarized by that crucial afternoon in the 1940s when Borges and Cortázar, the ultimate esthete and the doubtful ideologue, met. The two writers have come to symbolize the nation's two distinctive ways of writing; literature as intellectual exercise and literature as playful, philosophical game and as political investigation. The attention they have received abroad, however, is not equal. Alongside Vladimir Nabokov, Luigi Pirandello, Italo Calvino, and Friedrich Dürrenmatt, the former is considered today a master of the twentieth century, a first-rate fabulist to be read endlessly. His bookish essays and stories—"The Aleph," "Tlön Uqbar, orbis tertius," and "The Garden of Forking Paths" among them—are the best known and have been elevated to the status of classics. The latter, on the other hand, although active as a writer since 1951, is eclipsed today in his own home, Latin America, as well as in Europe and the United States. While a number of scholarly studies on Cortázar have been published in the past couple of decades, in the United States his oeuvre, after an initial explosion of interest, has ceased to attract the type of attention granted to him in the late 1960s and throughout the 1970s. His sudden death of leukemia in 1984, at age 69, mysterious at the time and rumored to be AIDS-related, and the passing of an era of free-spirited youthfulness in international writing, have pushed Cortázar to an obscure corner. Borges now reigns almost alone, unaccompanied by his compatriot. But now that a reevaluation of the 1960s as a rite of passage, a crucial turning point in recent history, is at hand, Cortázar's art needs to be revisited, his aesthetics and ideology reassessed.

Banfield

A contemporary of Octavio Paz, the Nobel prize–winning Mexican poet and essayist with whom he would occasionally collaborate and who would write a moving obituary at the time of his death, Julio Florencio Cortázar was born in Brussels on 26 August 1914, at the start of World War I. Cortázar was born into a middle-class milieu, but his family tree is full of itinerant travelers: his father was a descendant of immigrants from the Basque province in Spain,[3] and his maternal lineage is traceable to France and Germany. Europe, Cortázar's birth place, would stimulate more than transient passion in him, regardless of his Argentine descent: it would play an important role throughout his life, becoming his permanent address from the moment he turned 37, when Peronism pushed him out of the Southern Hemisphere. As it happened, when he was born, his father, also called Julio Cortázar, was temporarily stationed in Brussels as a specialist in economic affairs attached to the Argentine embassy there. The family remained in Brussels until 1918, when, after a short visit to Spain, they returned to their native Argentina.

The Cortázar family settled in Banfield, the lower-middle-class suburb of urban Buenos Aires, where "The Poison" ("Los venenos") and some other future stories of his would take place. Located in the southern section of the city, not far from a famous slaughterhouse immortalized in a classic tale by Esteban Echeverría written in the early decades of the nineteenth century, Banfield was known as an industrial and manufacturing district. It was heavily contaminated. Factory chimneys dotted the landscape wherever you looked. Banfield had dusty, unpaved streets, and in the early 1920s, when Cortázar was a child, horses still prevailed as one, although not the only, means of transportation.

His parents' difficult marriage and ultimate separation marked Cortázar deeply. When he was six his father abandoned the family. He would not know a thing about his father until news of the elder Cortázar's death, in the Cordoba province of Argentine, arrived many years later. Although emotionally devastated, even in his adult life he would never talk about the split, as if its insurmountable pain needed to remain forever private. Paternal figures populate his fiction—for instance, in the allegorical novel *The Winners* (1960; *Los premios*), about a group of civilians awarded as a lottery prize a boat cruise and are suddenly left unattended at sea, without a captain to guide their boat, in the form of quasi-divine figures and incognito authoritarian rules who control in absentia individual lives, manipulating them as marionettes. The novel is obviously a parable on tyranny and anarchy, and the character of the capricious leader recalls Cortázar's disappearing father.

Cortázar and his sister, Ofelia, one year his junior and his only sibling, were raised by his mother and by an aunt in a larger-than-usual house—one with a large backyard, numerous rooms, and obscure, empty corners that became the model of "House Taken Over."[4] Cortázar and his sister developed a complicated relationship with incestuous undertones, which he also often refused to discuss in interviews. But, once again, his oeuvre, although never to be taken at face value in its biographical information, may serve as map: in a number of early short stories, including "House Taken Over" and "Bestiary," incest is indeed a crucial issue. In the former tale, Irene, the female protagonist, has rejected two potential husbands to live alone in a family house with her male sibling, whose girlfriend, María Esther (María was the name of Cortázar's mother), died just before they were to be engaged. Brother and sister inhabit the place as a functional loving couple, convinced it is their duty to carry on the genealogical legacy of safeguarding the place. "We liked the house," the narrator claims, "because, apart from its being old and spacious (in a day when old houses go down for a profitable auction of their construction materials), it kept the memories of great-grandparents, our paternal grandfather, our parents and the whole of childhood."[5] They live intimately, almost like husband and wife:

> Whenever Irene talked in her sleep, I woke up immediately and stayed awake. I never could get used to this voice from a statue or a parrot, a voice that came out of the dreams, not from a throat. Irene said that in my sleep I flailed about enormously and shook the blankets off. We had the living room between us, but at night you could hear everything in the house. We heard each other breathing, coughing, could even feel each other reaching for the light switch

when, as happens frequently, neither of us could fall asleep. *(Blow-Up,* 15)

Notwithstanding the siblings' explicit attachment, no incestuous act is ever described in any direct manner in "House Taken Over." Cortázar's tale, set in Argentina in the late 1940s, while the two-times dictator Juan Domingo Perón (1946–55 and 1973–74), a right-wing populist, was first in office, is more about external powers overwhelming the house and its inhabitants than anything else. The reader is invited to witness the fashion in which a tyrannical regime slowly takes over the daily routine of its citizens: it consumes their mental and physical energy and reduces their behavior to unfree, besieged mechanical acts. The two protagonists, Irene and the unnamed narrator, go from enjoying their whole house to living in a single, tiny room because an undescribed absolute force has taken over the rest of the building. Imprisonment is the key word. I shall return to this political dimension in "House Taken Over" later on; it is enough to say for now that the siblings become prisoners in their own habitat. Are they forced to an intimacy they would otherwise not choose to embrace? Perhaps. They do nurture an undeniable need for each other, an incestuous dependency, but there is no question that outside forces make them even closer.

The other story purportedly about incest, "Bestiary," a surrealist tale with obvious psychoanalytic undertones recalling Luis Buñuel's early films *L'Age d'or* and *Le chien andalou* (1930), is about a tiger who lives freely in the Funes mansion. Isabel, a young girl visiting her relatives, has hidden desires toward her Aunt Rema. The feline roams the maze of rooms regulating the lives of its inhabitants, but everybody accepts its presence, although a warning has been put out to prevent running into it in the house. The members of the cast are Rema and Luis, their boy Nino, and Luis's brother, the Kid. Isabel, through letters to her mother, shows an aversion for the Kid. At one point she seizes the opportunity to misinform him of the tiger's whereabouts. Hiding her face in her accomplice Aunt Rema's skirt, she hears the Kid's dying screams.[6]

So, should one infer from these stories that Cortázar had an incestuous relationship with his sister? Keeping with the confessional spirit of the time, in interviews Cortázar acknowledged having had a recurrent dream of sleeping in the same bed with Ofelia. At the same time, nonincestuous fraternal relationships also abound in his oeuvre. They play a major role in "Letters from Mama" ("Cartas de mamá"), "End of the Game" ("Final del juego"), and "Letter to a Young Lady in Paris" ("Carta a una señorita en París"), to be discussed later on in this section.

Life in Banfield was intriguing: Cortázar was curious and bookish, always intellectually driven, with an unconventional point of view, which often scared young friends and made him a loner, a sort of pariah and pushing him to the fringes of society. The neighborhood was the playground where he tasted the sweet innocence of childhood. In it he discovered insects (ants, spiders, flies, bees), a quintessential presence in his short fiction, and had his first encounters with death and romantic disillusionment. These three elements—love, death, and insects—are incorporated into "The Poison," an enchanting story, unavailable in English, to be read vis-à-vis Kafka's "The Metamorphosis" (1915), Calvino's "The Argentine Ant" (1976), and William H. Gass's "Order of Insects" (1981).[7] The tale is based on real experiences. When Cortázar was seven his cat, Pituco, was found dead one morning, after eating poison set out for ants invading the kitchen. Deeply saddened, he buried it in his own garden[8] and, many years later, transformed memory into art. In "The Poison" a nameless Argentine boy living in Banfield in an unspecified home welcomes his uncle, Don Carlos, after the latter acquires a device, a unique machine, to exterminate ants. The child is anxious to see it function. A terrible battle against the ever-multiplying ants has been unsuccessful at his home so far, and this may well be the final effort. Cortázar never offers a detail description of the insect protagonist, not even an ambiguous one like Kafka's. "We knew quite well those ants of Banfield," he said, "the black ants that slowly devour everything, making anthills on the sand, in squares, throughout the mysterious piece of land where a house sinks into the center of the earth. It's there where they make concealed holes but are unable to hide the black line that goes and comes bringing bits of leaves" (quoted in Garfield 1975, 22). What is intriguing is how routine continues unaffected while ants slowly build an alternative reality beneath Banfield's surface—in its underground they establish a trait complex of labyrinthine paths away from the light of day, interconnecting one home with another, one garden with the next. Uncle Carlos's device to annihilate the intolerable foe bombs insecticide into holes through a wind hose. As a result, ants, supposedly, will automatically perish by the millions.

If anything, the story is invaluable in its portrait of Cortázar's early life in Banfield. Soon the problem is elevated to a larger-than-life struggle between order and chaos, progress and fatality, civilization and barbarism. As it develops, however, the tale is also concerned with the coming of age of the intelligent, active boy protagonist, involved with books and girls. He loves Lila, who in turn is infatuated with Hugo, turning him into a rival. Everything he sees is described in terms of folk heroes (e.g., Sitting Bull) and comic strips (*Billiken*, Raffles, the equivalent of Dick Tracy, The Shadow, Superman), which allows us to penetrate, albeit obliquely, the writer's mind while still young. The narrator satirizes technology and loves humor. Indeed, in no time Don Carlos's poison begins to affect plantations in nearby sections and, when inhaled, upsets the psyche of neighbors, driving them crazy. By annihilating ants, the boy is able to take revenge against Lila for her unpardonable betrayal. He therefore manages to become a winner, at least in his own imagination. While "The Poison" is no masterpiece, its voice reflects Cortázar's intellectual development and precociousness. As in the story, his own universe, peaceful on its surface, was full of fear and unrecognized violence.

Psychosomatics

In 1937 an uncertified doctor recommended to Cortázar's mother that the child, an avid reader and frequent dreamer, stay away from books since they could affect his health. Fortunately for Cortázar, the prescription was ignored. He loved radio, commercial films, and Greek mythology. He especially enjoyed reading about adventurous heroes traveling to distant places. Not surprisingly, his favorite writer was Jules Verne, and he is said to have read *Twenty Thousand Leagues under the Sea* (1870), a romance about submarines with Captain Nemo as its villain, several times. He wanted to be a sailor and navigate distant seas. "I will always be a child in many ways," he once wrote, "but one of those children who from the beginning carries within an adult, so when the little monster becomes an adult he carries in turn a child inside and, *nel mezzo del camino*, yields to the seldom peaceful coexistence of at least two outlooks onto the world."[9]

His multicultural genealogical tree (part South American, part Basque, French, German, and Belgian) resulted in a polyglot education. He spoke fluent French during his boyhood, and his library—described in passing in "Letter to a Young Lady in Paris"—then, as in the years to come, consisted mainly of foreign titles, specially Francophone and Anglo-Saxon. (Borges had a similar upbringing: in part a descendant of British immigrants, English was used at home, a language in which he is said to have first read *Don Quixote*. When time came to find the Spanish original, he was sure he had mistaken it for a poor translation.)[10] In order to help support the household, at 18 he received a degree as a secondary-school teacher and taught for a decade, from 1935 to 1945, in several Buenos Aires provinces, including Bolívar and Chivilcoy. The job had both drawbacks and benefits. After his classroom hours, he would spend most of his free time completely alone, which made him miserable, especially because there was virtually no intellectual atmosphere in those provincial communities. On the other hand, he had an enormous amount of time to read and pushed himself into ambitious bibliographical projects: for instance, in a few months he read Sigmund Freud's oeuvre and the work of the Spanish critic and lexicographer Ramón Menéndez y Pelayo. According to critic Terry J. Peavler, it was during the Bolívar and Chivilcoy period that Cortázar developed neurotic symptoms he would later on use as inspiration in his short fiction.[11] As theme or leitmotiv, neurosis appears in "Axolotl," "Letter to a Young Lady in Paris," "The Other Heaven," "The Distances," "The Health of the Sick," and numerous other tales. His characters suffer from this mild form of mental disorder: they are intensely and inappropriately fearful of things and situations and compulsively need to pursue certain thoughts or actions in order to reduce anxiety. They have such physical symptoms as tenseness, fatigue, and the excessive use of defense mechanisms, and these neurotic aspects are frequently pushed to limit, becoming forms of psychosis, which involve a loss of the sense of reality. In his short stories Cortázar is careful enough never to discuss these mental disturbances and ailments in Freudian terms; he shied away from psychoanalysis (as did Borges), trusting that any hallucination, any form of psychological sickness, ought to be understood, perhaps even overcome, through the best treatment: literature. It would indeed be easy to reduce Cortázar's complex work to mere psychosomatic contrivances, but by doing so its artistic power would be altogether lost.

Add to it Cortázar's overwhelming physical presence, which often frightened his peers. He was a very tall, around six feet six inches, an anomaly for a Latin American. José Lezama Lima, the Cuban novelist who wrote *Paradiso* (1966), used to say that Cortázar had received the gift of eternal youth in exchange for never being able to stop growing taller. His summer house in Saignon, France, had to be remodeled in order for him to fit in the kitchen and bathrooms. Years later, in Paris, he met the Colombian journalist and later Nobel prize winner Gabriel García Márquez, who admired Cortázar's early work. They met in October 1956 at the Old Navy Café on the Boulevard Saint-Germain. He was "like an apparition," said the author of *Love in the Time of Cholera* (1985). Cortázar "was the tallest man you could possibly imagine, wearing a voluminous black raincoat which was more like the dark cloak of a widow. His face was the face of a perverse child: wide-set eyes like those of a heifer, so oblique and filmy they might have seemed diabolical had they not been submitted to the domination of the heart."[12]

His height, nevertheless, seems not to have made him uncomfortable. Never physically handicapped, his characters are always prisoners of their mental machinations, not their bodies. As friends described him, he was punctilious, affable, straightforward, whimsical, lanky, and freckled.[13] José Donoso, the Chilean author of *Curfew* (1983), used to describe him as very introspective and reserved. "He hides behind a curtain of friendliness and courtesy," he observed. "People say he doesn't accept or offer intimacy. Friends that loved him and admired him for various and valuable reasons told me they would never go to him in times of crisis. They would never speak to him about their problems, and neither did Julio [speak to them about his]."[14] Luis Harss portrays him as follows: "a true Argentine, [he] is a many-sided man, culturally eclectic, elusive in person, mercurial in his ways. There is something adamantly neat and precise about him. . . . There is a child in his eyes. He looks much too young for his age. In fact, his generally boyish air is almost unsettling. An eternal child prodigy keeps winking at us from his work" (Harss, 209).

Wrestling to Be Born

Argentina, since its independence, has been a stage for political instability and military coups—and the twentieth century is no exception. In 1945 the country belatedly entered World War II on the Allies' side after four years of pro-Allied neutrality. Juan Domingo Perón, an army colonel who, with a group of military colleagues, seized power a year before, won the elections in 1946 and established a popular dictatorship with the support of the army, nationalists, and the Roman Catholic Church. He remained in power until 1955 and developed a following among workers, clergymen, landowners, and industrialists. He instituted a program of revolutionary measures that were supposed to lead to economic self-sufficiency. Around the time Cortázar taught courses in French literature— mainly Mallarmé and Baudelaire, his two idols at the time—at the University of Cuyo, Mendoza, he was active in a resistance aganst Perón. He was even arrested and freed shortly thereafter. The incident made it clear a dismissal from his academic job was imminent and, thus, Cortázar resigned his position and returned to Buenos Aires. His opposition to Perón's regime and his overall political participation was passive at best. He considered himself an esthete— an intellectual involved with ideas and unconcerned with the daily struggle to overthrow a dictatorship, even one in his own country. He advocated art for art's sake, intellectual freedom, and, much like the early Rubén Darío, a crucial Nicaraguan figure in the Modernista movement that swept Latin America from 1885 to 1915, identified himself with the romantic idea of the poet living in an ivory tower—isolated, away from the discomfort of mundane affairs.

This attitude colored Cortázar's beginnings as a writer: his role, he believed, was to discuss and entertain, to perceive reality objectively from afar. Still, however, Peronism is important as a ghost in his short fiction. Once again, "House Taken Over" is the best example to study this dimension. In interviews he related the beginning of the tale as a nightmare he once had, in which he was alone in a house full of passageways when, suddenly, a noise was heard from the depths of a corridor. A sense of terror overwhelmed him. After quickly closing the door, then bolting it tight, for a few minutes Cortázar felt safe. The nightmare had become a peaceful dream, he thought. But suddenly, as a noise sounded on his side of the door, he woke quickly and, still in his pajamas, sat down at the typewriter. In an hour an a half the text was ready.[15] And although the plot to him had "absolutely no other meaning than that of a nightmare" (quoted in Garfield 1975, 19), critics like Jaime Concha, Juan Carlos Curuchet, and Joaquín Roy have studied its hidden meanings.[16]

As mentioned before, the text can essentially be read as a political comment on Perón's dictatorial regime and his infiltration of everything Argentine. Irene and her brother, who support themselves from the rental of properties the family has owned for generations in the provinces, slowly become victims of an abstract force devoted to taking away parts of their beloved house. Of course, as Borges and Cortázar himself claim, "House Taken Over" is also a supernatural tale—that is, a ghost story with abstract, nonpolitical connotations. And other entries in *Bestiary*, including "Omnibus," a tantalizing description of a bumpy bus ride through downtown Buenos Aires, can also be read as a critique of Peronism. Clara, a nurse, rides the same bus Cortázar used to take to work in Buenos Aires. A fragile woman, she feels attacked by the hostile glances of the other passengers, all of whom carry flowers, and even by the conductor, who lunges at her several times. The ride is dangerous. At one point the driver stops abruptly to let the passengers be dropped at the cemetery—obviously a reference to Argentina's slow agony under the populist tyrant and an insinuation that perhaps the passengers carry their own flowers because they are visiting their own graves. Death is a silent partner. At any rate, the ony other omnibus passenger who doesn't have a bouquet of flowers, a young man, sympathizes with Clara, and the couple suddenly acquire an aura of rebellion. They symbolize, and are viewed as, an anti-establishment voice. Consequently, they are ostracized, turned into enemies of the people, suspicious citizens. At the end Clara and her companion manage to escape the conductor's reckless driving through the slamming doors into the plaza, departing from the vehicle's suicidal rendezvous.

Intellectually speaking, Borges already commanded a major influence on Argentine cultural life when Cortázar was in his late twenties. He had published *A Universal History of Infamy* in 1935, and in the next few years, after a near-fatal accident, would produce outstanding short stories like "Pierre Menard, Author of the *Quixote*." His precise, almost mathematical style had a small but fanatical following in the city's intellectual circles and his reviews in Victoria Ocampo's literary magazine, *Sur*, were eagerly awaited every month. Cortázar, to be sure, admired Borges, but he also found him dry and pedantic (snobbish?). At the time he discovered another crucial literary figure to be attracted to: Roberto Arlt,[17] a Buenos Aires crime reporter and anarchist whose remarkable sequence of urban nightmares—*The Rabid Toy, Seven Madmen*, and *The Flame-throwers*, published in 1926, 1929, and 1931, respectively—were sold for only a few cents at newsstands.

Borges and Arlt were artistic opposites: while the former was known as a crafter of overly sophisticated fiction using—perhaps abusing—bibliographical references and philosophical quotes, the latter was a careless stylist in close touch with the metropolitan masses. Arlt's characters are often anarchists with eccentric ideas, people plotting to destabilize the status quo; unable to control their instincts, they run amok and end up destroying themselves. The differences between the two illuminates the way the Argentine intelligentsia was divided at the time in two major groups, irrevocable rivals in their esthetic approach: Florida and Boedo, named after the location of cafés where members of each group used to meet to chat about literature and politics. Cortázar identified with the author of "Approach to Almotasim" but was infatuated with Arlt's adventurous plots and his use of *lunfardo*, Argentina's urban slang.[18] Eventually, he would oscillate between one pole and the other, becoming a secret disciple of Borges while, also, constantly paying tribute to his other major influence, Arlt, by drafting stories where characters look for existential answers in their convoluted, violent urban environment, as in the case of "Friends" ("Los Amigos"), an account of three former friends who have become active in an anarchist terrorist group (the third friend has been ordered by the first to kill the second—a mission he carries out effectively): it is a tale like any in *The Rabid Toy*. Besides, Cortázar's style, although carefully constructed, uses Arlt's fabulous spontaneous verbosity and rhythmic improvisation.

Cortázar later moved back to Buenos Aires, back to his mother, sister, and aunt, and began working as a manager of Cámara Argentina del Libro, a government-run printing association. More or less simultaneously he applied, was accepted, and registered in the Department of Arts and Letters at the University of Buenos Aires but would never finish a degree. At the age of 24, under the pseudonym Julio Denis, he embarked on a young writer's dream to self-publish his first booklet of poems, *Presencia* (Presence), a collection of Mallarmean sonnets about which he would have little to say later on. While Peronism was at its peak, Cortázar met José Bianco, Victoria Ocampo, and other Argentina intellectuals, and began writing reviews and short essays for *Sur*, the most prestigious journal of ideas of the southern cone, to which numerous writers of international fame contributed between 1931 and 1970, including Roger Caillois, Waldo Frank, and Hermann de Keyserling.[19] Many of Cortázar's critical texts in the journal, while collected in his three-volume *Obra crítica* (1994), are little known and almost forgotten. They are important in that they trace his intellectual journey, as well as his literary influences, perhaps better than anything he would create thereafter. Aside from *Sur*, at the time he also wrote for such other magazines as *Cabalgata* and *Realidad*. All together, these texts on Graham Greene's *The Heart of the Matter*, on Cyril Connolly, André Gide, Eugene O'Neill, Søren Kierkegaard, and Aldous Huxley, and on Luis Buñuel's 1950 film *Los olvidados* are a compass as to the direction in which Cortázar as novelist and short-story writer would take his talent.

The invitation to write for *Sur* in particular couldn't have come at a better moment. More than anything else, it meant somehow to be related to Borges and his acolytes, to enter the master's circle of close collaborators. But Cortázar's style and concerns immediately distinguished him from the Borgesian galaxy. In 1948, for instance, he contributed to the magazine an obituary to Antonin Artaud,[20] considered today the first text in which he expressed his views on surrealism, a philosophical and artistic movement he was infatuated with, which left a deep mark on him, and whose promoters—André Breton, Tristan Tzara, et al.—he admired. He had become acquainted as well with Francisco Ayala, a Spanish émigré who at the time was editing *Realidad*. "The vast Surrealist experiment," he wrote in 1949 in Ayala's magazine, "seems to me the highest enterprise modern man has embarked upon in an attempt to find an integrated humanism. At the same time, the surrealist attitude (inclined to the liquidation of genres and species) colors the verbal and plastic creation, incorporating to the movement an irrational element."[21] Cortázar wrote for Ayala not only essays on Breton and Artaud but also his first overly ambitious essay on the contemporary movel,[22] and a bit later he contributed a review of Leopoldo Marechal's *Adam Buenosayres*,[23] a voluminous novel considered a classic today but at the time attacked as artistic trash because of its Argentine author's loyalties to Peronism.

Putting politics aside, Cortázar celebrated Marechal's style and intelligence and applauded his portrait of national urban life. The review created a small scandal of sorts in Buenos Aires. Cortázar received death threats and was accused of collaborating with the enemy. The Marechal affair, notwithstanding, offered Cortázar a type of exposure, an early recognition he was anxious to get in intellectual circles. The incident also illuminates his patriotic pride, which he made crystal clear in a couple of tales about tango and boxing, including "Return Trip Tango" and "Torito," the latter based on the historical figure Luis Angel Firpo (aka El Toro Salvaje de la Pampa), an Argentine heavyweight boxing champ who lost his title to Jack Dempsey at Madison Square Garden in 1923. A study of the macho spirit in South America, the story begins in the hospital where Torito is immobilized after being defeated by Víctor Peralta upon his return to Buenos Aires. In *lunfardo*, he recalls his life to a friend listening near his bed. Born into a lower-class family in the *arrabal* La Quemada, Torito confesses that while he fought in the Argentine, he was honest and clean. But once he began a career overseas, things drasticaly changed. He claims he lost to Dempsey because of his refusal to accept, even at the request of his own coach, corrupt boxing codes, especially in New York. Cortázar's text is not about flags, anthems, and nationalistic memorabilia but about courage and Argentina's difficulty adapting to outside ethical standards.

Patriotism is also an issue in the small gem of a story "The Band" ("La banda"), a confession that takes place in 1947 and is dedicated to René Crevel. Lucio Medina, a film aficionado, tells Cortázar, the author and narrator, the humorous plot. Years before he left Argentina, forever giving up his career and possessions, he claims, he went to the Grand Opera Theater to see a film by Anatole Litvak announced in the local paper. But instead of the movie, he got a band of ridiculous teenagers: Banda de Alpargatas, a group of Perón-sympathizing cheerleaders. Medina couldn't believe his ears and for a while thought he had landed in the wrong theater. He quietly sat in the audience, thinking the absurd act was only a quick preview to Litvak's art, but the band kept on playing one terrible song after another. Bewildered, oversaturated, and furious, he eventually stood up and left the place, thinking he had been a victim of the "official culture." But days later he realized the event had a larger-than-life meaning: the band he heard was a symbol of the sort of national idiosyncrasy he was fed up with. Anxious and existentially confused, he decided to abandon the country.

If anything, "The Band" is an explanation of Cortázar's own animosity toward Peronist culture and an early explanation of why he chose exile as a form of life.

By 1951, when he reached 37, his apprenticeship was over. Cortázar's views on fiction-versus-reality, on nationalism, on the role of the intellectual in Latin America, were formed. Although he had begun writing novels, he understood the short story as the most valuable tool to explore his own neurosis and that of South America. He also understood that it is a difficult genre to master: you have to be brief and put the right word in the right place; your reader will expect to finish the text in one sitting, which means the reader's attention span is short and precious. As he would testify in the essay "On the Short Story and Its Environs," Cortázar soon realized that his challenge in short fiction was to find the peculiar and bizarre in the most routinely—to intertwine dreams and reality. To succeed, he would need to find ways to disappear as the author, to be detached, to bring the surreal into daily life. As he put it in the essay, "I know I have always been irritated by stories in which the characters have to wait in the wings while the narrator exploits details or developments from one situation to another." He added, "For me the thing that signals a great story is what we might call its autonomy, the fact that it detaches itself from its author like a soap bubble blown from a clay pipe."

Pulp Fiction

Up until recently it was widely believed that Cortázar began his career as a novelist in the mid-1940s, but he had in fact burned a 600-page manuscript written before then and was unable to find a publisher for a second novel, *The Exam* (*El examen*), about student life in Buenos Aires, which would be published posthumously. The appearance in Spain, in 1994, of his multivolume collected works (*Obras completas*) signals a different path. We now know that between 1937 and 1945 a full-length volume of tales, *La otra orilla* (The Other Shore), unavailable in English, was finished in the province of Mendoza. It opened with an epigraph by Matthew Arnold ("And we are here on a darkling plain / Swept with confused alarms of struggle and flight, / Where ignorant armies clash by night"), and in a brief *nota bene* a young Cortázar claims he has collected the stories, scattered in separate drawers, to conclude a creative period and begin a new and, it was hoped, purer one. The volume is then divided into three large sections: *Plagios y traducciones* (Plagiarisms and Translations), *Historias de Gabriel Medrano* (Stories of Gabriel Medrano), and *Prolegómenos a la astrología* (Prolegomena to Astrology). The unifying themes are vampires, neurotic characters, playful minimalist instructions, and the fantastic. Indeed, as Terry J. Peavler has shown, Cortázar wrote for many years, polishing his craft, before he began to publish stories in earnest (Peavler, 23). Several novice tales, reworked from *La otra orilla*—including "Estación de la mano" (Season of the Hand), about a mysterious hand that visits the first-person narrator, falls in love with his left hand, and makes him cut it off so they can be together, and "La caricia más profunda" (The Most Profound Caress), about a man who is slowly sinking into the ground to the point where he disappears altogether—later on appeared in his nonfiction books, especially *Historias de cronopios y de famas (Cronopios and Fames)*, as well as *Ultimo round* and *La vuelta al día en ochenta mundos*, collected in English translation under the title *Around the Day in Eighty Worlds*. The fact that they remained unknown can be attributed to the writer's difficulty in finding a publisher or to his self-doubts as an artist. He was 31 at the time and

21

although full of future projects, didn't quite feel secure about his talent and technique.

It is symptomatic that Cortázar chose the terms *plagiarism* and *translations* to describe some of the entries: the bulk of the entries of *La otra orilla* are immature, half-baked, and can be read as forgettable tributes to Lovecraft and Poe, as poorly conceived screenplays for B-movies of the horror genre, à la Ed Wood. In one, "El hijo del vampiro" (The Vampire's Son), a woman beaten by a vampire gets pregnant and gives birth to a monstrous child while simultaneously undergoing a metamorphosis that makes her disappear. In another, "Llama el teléfono, Delia" (The Phone Is Ringing, Delia), an estranged husband, a good-for-nothing, calls his wife to talk, ask for forgiveness, and says good-bye before he departs on a long trip. Hours later, Delia, the wife, finds out he couldn't have called her because at the time of the conversation we was already dead, shot in street. The style is unquestionably Cortázar's, but the themes and characters seem mere silhouettes—raw, unfinished.

Four years later, in 1949, Cortázar published, with his friend Daniel Devoto's money, a theatrical piece (or, as he called it, a dramatic poem): the highly polished *Los reyes* (The Kings), based on the myth of Minotaur. As Evelyn Picon Garfield and others have argued, the book, which remained among his favorites until the end, is a cornerstone in his literary career. In the Greek myth, Minos, king of Crete, promises to sacrifice to the gods a white bull sent to him by Neptune. But when he tries the trick of sacrificing another bull, Neptune seeks revenge by making Minos's wife fall in love with the animal. The Minotaur—half-bull, half-human—is the result of their union. Minos imprisons the Minotaur in a labyrinth and feeds him with seven men and seven women every seven years. When Theseus, a future victim, is about to be sacrificed, Ariadne, Minos's daughter, falls in love with him. She gives Theseus a sword, and he penetrates the labyrinth and kills the Minotaur, perceived as an aggressive ogre.

Cortázar's version, on the other hand, defends the Minotaur, who is made to represent freedom. Ariadne, in love with the monster, masterminds a plot in which Theseus battles the Minotaur but dies. As the true hero of the tale, the Minotaur leaves the labyrinth to seek the company of Ariadne. Although *Los reyes* hardly received any positive critical attention (Enrique Anderson Imbert, author of an encyclopedic study of Latin American letters, did praise it at the time), it embodies Cortázar's peculiar worldview, where pariahs have a unique perspective on reality and thus are more likely to unravel the secrets of the universe. The minotaur is a symbol of instinctive desire and of "otherness," a dreamlike figure inhabiting a region frequented by the writer's future characters: reality in reverse. By defending otherness, Cortázar celebrates the individual versus the collective—that is, the peculiar versus the conventional.

Its plot is reminiscent of "Moebius Strip," among the most tantalizing of Cortázar's political stories and, according to Terry J. Peavler, his "most troubling, most unpalatable" (Peavler, 30). "Moebius Strip" is about a young British schoolteacher on a bicycle tour of France who is raped and killed by a man she encounters in a forest. Surprisingly, Janet, the victim, enjoys her suffering. She is murdered by Robert, her attacker, not because she struggles but because she wants him to use precaution so as not to get pregnant. After the violent scene, the action moves forward in time to the moment Robert awaits execution for his crime, at which point Janet's spirit returns and, ignited by sexual desire, visits him in his cell. He then commits suicide and Janet waits for him to revive so they can consummate their passion. As in *Los reyes*, Cortázar's two characters are outcasts who need to escape the labyrinths of life to reunite. Critics in general, and feminists in particular, have of course attacked "Moebius Strip" as a senseless, outrageous tale, arguing that while its technique and poetic style make the reader at times forget its nefarious content, the plot hides a troublesome element of atrociousness and looks for pleasure in an acknowledged criminal act, as happens in Cortázar's 1949 dramatic poem.

Throughout the 1940s, Cortázar, a high-brow intellectual, spent a considerable amount of his time reading pulp fiction. It was not an unusual interest; his entire generation inherited from the adventures of British armchair detectives the passion for literature as sleuth. Indeed, besides Mallarmé, Keats, Baudelaire, and other romantics, among Cortázar's adolescent passions in the spirit of the time, was police and crime fiction. It was common at the time and thereafter that a number of publishing houses in Buenos Aires would invest in thrillers and some even contracted luminaries like Borges and the novelist Ricardo Piglia, author of *Respiración artificial* (1981; *Artificial Respiration*), to direct special series like El Séptimo Círculo. More than any other Latin American country, including Mexico, Argentina embraced the tradition of detective, dime, and hard-boiled novels wholeheartedly.[24] Not only was the subgenre highly commercial, it was also embraced by the sophisticated elite. Aside from writing "Death and the Compass,"

Borges, together with his longtime collaborator Adolfo Bioy Casares, published his collection *Six Problems for Isidro Parodi* (1942), humorous detective tales that mock urban jargon and social manners. And one year later the team brought out *The Best Detective Stories*, an anthology that displayed the subgenre in its most coolly intellectual forms. Cortázar read every high-brow and cheap thriller available, and in his words, became "an expert on the detective story" (Garfield 1978, 92).

Together with a friend, he prepared a comprehensive bibliography on every thriller available in Spanish, to be published in the *Revista de bibliotecología*, sponsored by the University of Buenos Aires. They came up with the pseudonym Morton Heinz, supposedly a distinguished British criminologist in charge of the bibliography. Their research was tremendous: they began with Edgar Allan Poe and continued with Willard Huntington Wright (aka S. S. Van Dine), Ellery Queen, and John Dickson Carr. Cortázar was particularly enchanted with Edgar Wallace, an English writer, widely popular in the River Plate, who wrote some 200 novels, among them *Captains of Souls*, which, in essence, carries the seed of "The Distances" ("Lejana"): a villain implicates an honest man in a crime, and when he attends his execution, a transmigration takes place in which the villain is actually punished. In Cortázar's story Alina Reyes, a young woman living in Buenos Aires, becomes obsessed with a recurrent vision of her double, a beggar woman in Budapest. She experiences the beggar's hardships when she herself should be happy; increasingly the hallucination becomes a reality. Through her diary the reader witnesses Alina's psychological deterioration. At one point, for example, she is tormented by the beatings her Budapest counterpart suffers; she feels her cold and slowly begins to inhabit the other woman's life. The transmutation ends when Alina travels to Eastern Europe on her honeymoon, which she concocted to finally meet her double. An omniscient narrator relates the meeting of the two protagonists on a bridge as they embrace:

> Alina ached: it was the clasp of the pocketbook, the strength of the embrace had run it in between her breasts with a sweet, bearable laceration. She surrounded the slender woman feeling her complete and absolute within her arms, with a springing up of happiness equal to a hymn, to loosing a cloud of pigeons, to the river singing. She shut her eyes in the total fusion, declining the sensations from outside, the evening light; suddenly very tired but sure of her victory, without celebrating it as so much her own and at last. (*Blow-Up*, 27)

In a metamorphosis typical of Cortázar, similar to that described in "Axolotl," "The Other Heaven," "The Island at Noon," and "The Night Face Up," Alina becomes the other one, and vice versa. Dream and reality intertwine, exchanging positions. At the end, the Argentina character watches through the beggar's eyes. "Now she did scream," the text reads. "From the cold, because the snow was coming in through her broken shoes, because making her way along the roadway to the plaza went Alina Reyes, very lovely in her gray suit, her hair a little loose against the wind, not turning her face. Going off" (*Blow-Up*, 24).

While "The Distances" is not a detective story per se, it illuminates the influence of this popular subgenre in Cortázar's work, quite evident in "Continuity of Parks," a surprising metafictional thriller with a twist, Cortázar's most famous homage to dime novels. Set in an abstract, universal landscape, the three-page-long text is divided into two halves: in the first an anonymous reader (not unlike Cortázar's) is anxious to finish a thriller; he takes time off, boards a train, and travels to his weekend villa to continue enjoying the volume; in the second half a suspenseful plot describes a horse-riding man (no names are used) who promises his girlfriend to take revenge against a rival, probably someone competing for her love. She unsuccessfully tries to persuade him not to fight, but he decides to travel far and away, riding on a horse. He reaches a villa—the same villa where the reader, immersed in his book, is following the man's behavior: "He went up the three porch steps and entered. The woman's words reached him over the thudding of blood in his ears: first a blue chamber, then a hall, then a carpeted stairway. At the top, two doors. No one in the first room, no one in the second. The door of the salon, and then, the knife in the hand, the light from the great windows, the high back of an armchair covered in green velvet, the head of the man in the chair reading the novel" (*Blow-Up*, 65).[25]

Everywhere one finds pure mockery of pulp fiction: dogs, knives, passionate lovers, an enigma, an unknown victim—except that, in the metafictional tradition of Nabokov, Calvino, and Umberto Eco, the villain is the reader. In its structure, "Continuity of Parks" (unquestionably an unfortunate title) recalls a famous Borges essay, "Partial Enchantments of the *Quixote*," which discusses dramas and works of fiction where characters read themselves. Borges ends the piece with "Why does it make us uneasy to know that the map is within the map and the thousand and one nights are within *The Thousand and One Nights*?

Why does it disquiet us to know that Don Quixote is a reader of the *Quixote*, and Hamlet is a spectator of *Hamlet*? I believe I have found the answer: those inversions suggest that if the characters in a story can be readers or spectators, then we, their readers or spectators, can be fictitious. In 1833 Carlyle observed that universal history is an infinite sacred book that all men write and read and try to understand, and in which they too are written."[26] Actually, more than just the metafictional structure in Cortázar's text is reminiscent of Borges: its precise style and brevity is also familiar.

Another one of Cortázar's pulp-fiction thrillers is "El móvil" (The Motif), not available in English, about a *lunfardo*-speaking character from an *arrabal*, or poor neighborhood, who details his vengeance on the killer of his friend Montes. He penetrates the gang's spider web, uses prostitutes and alibis, until he meets his victim on a boat. The underlying objective, it is clear, is to render a plot reminiscent of Dashiell Hammett and Raymond Chandler, to make the dime novel subgenre an Argentine by-product. Cortázar's tale is particularly important because, while Borges and Bioy Casares were busy at the time mocking the British format of armchair detectives who are intellectually sophisticated and pedantic in nature, he was looking for inspiration elsewhere—Raymond Chandler's Philip Marlowe, and not Dorothy L. Sayers's Lord Peter Wimsey or Agatha Christie's Hercule Poirot, was his true model.[27]

Found in Translation

Cortázar earned a degree as a public translator and began working in that capacity for various Argentine publishing houses, including Argos and Imán, from 1945 to 1951. He translated G. K. Chesterton's *The Man Who Knew Too Much*, André Gide's *The Immoralist*, Daniel Defoe's *Robinson Crusoe*, Jean Giono's *The Birth of the Odyssey*, Louisa May Alcott's *Little Women*, and Marguerite Yourcenar's *Memoirs of Hadrian*, among other titles. He also embarked on an ambitious translation of the complete prose works of Edgar Allan Poe, a writer profoundly influential in his early career. A slow enterprise, the two-volume project on the author of *Eureka* (1848) and "The Purloined Letter" (1845) would not appear until 1956, under the aegis of the University of Puerto Rico and José Ortega y Gasset's magazine, *Revista de Occidente*. (Cortázar's future wife, Aurora Bernárdez, would help him accomplish the task and decades later would be the major force behind his multivolume *Complete Works*.) As a young man in his twenties, Cortázar had loved Rainer Maria Rilke's *Notebooks of Malte Lauris Brigge* (1910) but was now enamored with John Keats. Around 1946 he even published a now-forgotten essay on "Ode on a Grecian Urn"[28] and less than a 10 years later would embark on a Spanish translation of Lord Houghton's *Life and Letters of John Keats*.[29]

Critics like Rosario Ferré have studied Cortázar's romantic connection—his interest in making literature eccentric, unconventional, and rebellious. As she suggests, the American author of *Adventures of A. Gordon Pym* (1837) had a unique place in his heart. In retrospect, translating his prose oeuvre, more than anything else he did in the late 1940s, allowed him to shape his own style and build his own views on literature. While the politics of Chesterton and Gide, as well as Defoe's fabulations, can easily be traced in stories like "El móvil," "Moebius Strip," and "The Island at Noon" Poe became an everlasting influence. Titles and symbols have striking similarities: "The Fall of the House of Usher" and "House Taken Over," "The Distances" ("Lejana") and "Ligeia," "MS. Found in a Bottle" and "Manuscript Found in a Pocket," and so forth. But Poe's influence is far-reaching: most of

Cortázar's stories have an element of horror and the supernatural (e.g., the fantastic—an invitation to bizarre happenings), and a handful, including "Diary for a Story," are open tributes to the American author of "Facts in the Case of Mr. Valdemar."

Take the case of "The Distances" and of "Ligeia," which share a common thread: the Argentine story is about Alina Reyes's metamorphosis from a River Plate to a Hungarian woman, whereas Poe's 1838 tale has Ligeia, the narrator's mysterious dark-haired wife—a beautiful, wealthy, and scholarly woman—die in Germany after a lingering illness. After wandering around trying to forget, the narrator moves back to Britain and later marries Lady Rowena Trevanion, a woman he does not love. In the lavishly furnished English abbey to which they move, Rowena dies. Affected by opium, the narrator sees signs of life return to the corpse Finally Lady Rowena rises, transformed into Ligeia. Poe's drama of revivification deals with what the critic Kenneth Silverman calls "the revenant": a person (usually a woman) who returns from the "other world."[30] Alina Reyes also has a double, although hers is not dead but alive, across the Atlantic. Like Ligeia, she enters the psyche and body of the Budapest woman, thus becoming her other self. The geographic distance separating Argentina and Hungary can be read as the link between the Old World and the New, this world and the next.

Similarly, the Poe-Cortázar symbiosis can be traced in "The Other Heaven," considered a masterpiece by the Uruguayan scholar Emir Rodríguez Monegal. (My own opinion is less enthusiastic.)[31] Set in the Buenos Aires of the 1920s and the Paris of the 1860s, its male protagonist, a shy young Argentine stockbroker, does not dare approach the prostitutes of the Güemes Arcade. His double, nevertheless, has a satisfying liaison with a nineteenth-century French prostitute of the Galerie Vivienne. While the River Plate character is engaged to be married, through sights and odors he is able to travel back and finds a lover among the Paris prostitutes, but when he finally marries in Buenos Aires he no longer travels to Paris, his "other heaven." Quotations from Lautréamont's *Chants de Maldoror* are intertwined before every opening section, suggesting the boy is also a double of the "diabolic" Lautréamont, a contemporary of Rimbaud who lived and died in the same neighborhood. Finally, there is yet another fundamental character: Laurent, a murderer of prostitutes, like Jack the Ripper.

Terror and the bizarre, the double, past and present symmetries— the story brings forth the process of apprenticeship Cortázar underwent while translating Poe's fiction. Symmetries of past and present and the utopian desire to escape earthly existence are also found in "The Gates of Heaven." Marcelo and Mauro glimpse Mauro's dead wife, Celina, among the couples in her old hangout, a dance hall. She returns from the dead, and Mauro staggers across the dance floor after her, trying to find the gates of heaven among the smoke and multitude.

Also about doubles, and recalling Cortázar's translation of *Robinson Crusoe*, "The Island at Noon" is about Marini, an airline steward on commercial flights who often flies above the Aegean Sea. He lives a solitary life, a product of his busy schedule. His relationship with Carla, his companion, has ended, and he does nothing but devote himself to work. In his regular Rome-Teheran round trip, he flies over a tiny Greek island, Xiros, with which he becomes infatuated. He studies it from afar and carefully observes its primitive houses. While on the ground, he reads all about it in libraries. He uses every penny saved to travel to it and escape the mundane miseries of society. A utopian milieu, Xiros, with a population of 20, most of whom are related to Klaios and make a living from fishing octopus, is poor and unattended, but it is paradise in Marini's eyes. He hopes for a small room to feel absolutely happy, and he even devises ways to kill the former man that lived inside him, until he goes to the beach one day, takes off his watch, and is ready to sunbathe when he hears an explosion. The plane he had flown so many times has just crashed in front of him. He sees himself drowning and unsuccessfully tries to save his double. At the end his own corpse lies on the sand, surrounded by Xiros's inhabitants. The story is a frightening exercise in utopian and apocalyptic fiction: it examines the link between an individual's dreams and the capacity of fate to fulfill those dreams in a bizarre, fatal fashion.

Mutability

The year 1951 proved to be crucial in Cortázar's life. In opposition to the Peronist regime, he rejected a chair at the University of Buenos Aires and, almost simultaneously, was awarded a scholarship from the French government to study in Paris. Suddenly exile became an alternative he was happy to embrace. He thus moved to France, where he would live until his death more than 30 years later, dividing his time between a small Paris studio in the Latin Quarter and, later on, an apartment on Place du Général Beluret, and his summer home in Saignon, a town in the Vaucluse. While in Europe, he first worked for four months as a translator from French and English into Spanish for UNESCO but thereafter devoted himself fully to literature and his passions, boxing and the jazz trumpet. ("Torito" and "The Pursuer" utilize his knowledge of both.)

Exile in France seemed the best option for an avid reader, would-be writer, and polyglot with a perfect command of Voltaire's language. Away from Argentina, he would be able to explore his country's idiosyncrasy through fiction. Distance offers perspective, and perspective brings maturity. He would have time to meditate and read voraciously, an activity he adored. More than anything else, he would live at the center of culture, the apex of civilization—a fact very important since the depressing epoch when he taught secondary school in Bolívar and Chivilcoy. Deep at heart, Cortázar was tired of an existence on the periphery. Besides, there's an old saying among Latin American writers: "To be acclaimed at home, one first needs to be recognized abroad." He had been born in the Old World, where he received a cosmopolitan education during the first few years of his life; he was now anxious to return to his roots. Ironically, once in France, he began missing Argentina. Exile, he understood, is a universal state: every human is an island in an eternal diaspora. One lives constantly divided, neither here nor there. His language dilemma soon acquired difficult implications. To be exposed to another language on a daily basis, *to live* in another idiom, could eventually be detrimental to his work. His grammar and syntax were very much a part of the urban slang in the

River Plate. Like Roberto Arlt, he was deeply involved in recovering through literary tools the *arrabal* idiosyncrasy where *lunfardo* was spoken. Would he consider renouncing Spanish and writing in Rabelais's tongue? Could a literary career in two languages (i.e., two universes) be possible? Again, Borges served him as a useful paradigm. Borges's verbal style was unlike anything ever written in South America: a rigorous attack against arbitrariness, against clumsiness—an attempt to turn a Romance language into a meticulous artifact. If anything, Cortázar could inject the French flavor into his native tongue: make it laissez-faire. And indeed, after 1951, when the setting of his stories and novels expanded from Buenos Aires to Paris and to the world at large—Martinque, Cuba, Montevideo, Costa Rica, London, Nicaragua, and so forth—Argentina was turned into memory. A bridge between two cultures, neither here nor there, he would spend his life investigating the painful destiny of exile. Consequently, although he never defected from Spanish, the idiom in his stories, beginning with *End of the Game* (1956; revised 1964), is affected, artificial, foreign, and at times bookish—the product of a Robinson Crusoe isolated on his island, obsessed with remembering a lexicon he left behind with the shipwreck.

In 1951, in the same month Cortázar left for Paris, *Bestiary*, his first volume of stories containing eight entries, was published when the author was 37, by the respected Buenos Aires house Editorial Sudamericana. Together with his next two collections, it would be translated into English (although only in part) in 1963 and later published as *Blow-Up and Other Stories*.[32] Although, as with *Los reyes*, the reception was rather poor, this most impressive book would slowly become a favorite among young readers and critics, a true original in the Latin American tradition of short fiction. A number of scholars and critics, beginning in the late 1960s, have taken alternative roads to understanding it and Cortázar's short fiction esthetics in general.[33] They are divided as to how to interpret the *Bestiary* entries and have brought forth five different epistemological alternatives: as openly allegorical stories; as concerned with existential and social issues; as inheritors of the surrealist movement; as mythical; and as following what the Buenos Aires–based French critic Roger Caillois called "the fantastic"—that is, intertwining reality and dreams, often with a surprising horror twist.[34] Since this 1951 volume contains the seed of everything Cortázar would ever create, the same interpretative approaches apply for his future art.

Part 1

I prefer to divide his short fiction into two major categories: abstract, allegorical tales colored by the supernatural, which were written more or less uniformly until the late 1960s; and his political stories, deeply involved with violence, repression, human suffering, and, from 1968 on, the civilian and student unrest in Paris, Czechoslovakia, Mexico, Berkeley, and elsewhere. As I stated earlier, while the division might seem arbitrary at best, mainly because Cortázar kept on generating texts exemplifying the two categories, it is clear that his ideological commitment changed after the Cuban Revolution and as a result of his sympathy toward the 1979 Sandinista uprising in Nicaragua. "Apocalypse in Solentiname," part of *We Love Glenda So Much*, could only have been written in the late 1970s and early 1980s, not in Cortázar's early literary period, and a similar statement applies to "Press Clippings," part of the same collection. These stories offer a clear-cut understanding of Latin America's violence and political struggle, a result of the writer's new approach to his role as an intellectual responsible for denouncing collective crimes.

Exile made Cortázar incredibly prolific. Between 1956 and 1958 he published two other collections, bringing his stories to a total of 31. Juan José Arreola, the Mexican master storyteller who wrote *Confabulario* and was promoting a new literary generation that included José Emilio Pacheco and Salvador Elizondo, invited Cortázar to submit *End of the Game*, with nine entries, to Los Presentes, for a series under his directorship. The volume was published in 1956, and expanded with 18 more stories in 1964 in a Buenos Aires edition by Sudamericana. And a couple of years later, *Secret Weapons*, with five entries (considerably longer than Cortázar's earlier stories, averaging 30 to 40 pages), was published, also by Sudamericana, containing "Letters from Mama," "At Your Service," "Blow-Up," "The Pursuer," and "Secret Weapons." As a compact corpus, the 23 stories share a handful of common elements. First and foremost, they investigate the nature of childish games behind which a philosophical approach to life is hidden. The playful (in his own Spanish wording, *lo lúdico*) provides a constant theme throughout Cortázar's work, a sense of play offering an elaborate set of rules controlling human behavior. The approach, of course, extends to adulthood and often takes serious overtones. What the Argentine is suggesting is that behind our daily routine, behind what we call reality, another universe, richer yet chaotic, seductive yet fabulous, lies hidden ready to be seized. His objective is to invite the reader to unveil what at first sight looks like the quotidian: a trivial laughingstock,

32

a childish stratagem. In an interview in *Revista de la Universidad de México* Cortázar said, "In my case, the suspicion of another dimension of things, more secret and less communicable, and the fecund discovery of Alfred Jarry, for whom the true study of reality did not depend on the knowledge of its laws, but in the exception to such laws, have been some of the directing principles in my personal search for a literature at the margin of every naïve realism.[35] He did not populate his stories with fringe people—drunks, adulterers, unemployed and disturbed populace; and his style never relied on simplicity nor purported to be straightforward and functional. Anton Chekhov was his antimodel: the Russian's indirect, understated literary form, his affinity for understanding social and psychological types, was at the other extreme of Cortázar's artistic method; not routine but exception was the Argentine's theme, not realism but surrealism.

Take, for example, the charming "End of the Game." The story is about Letitia, Holanda, and the female narrator, three young girls who enjoy playing a ludicrous game. They go to the train tracks nearby, called the Argentine central tracks, and whenever a train passes, they turn themselves into funny human statues:

> Our kingdom was this: a long curve of the tracks ended its bend just opposite the back section of the house. There was just the gravel incline, the cross ties, and the double line of track; some dumb sparse grass among the rubble where mica, quartz and feldspar— the components of granite—sparkled like real diamonds in the two o'clock afternoon sun. When we stooped down to touch the rails (not wasting time because it would have been dangerous to spend much time there, not so much for the trains as for fear of being seen from the house), the heat off the stone roadbed flushed our faces, and facing into the wind from the river there was a damp heat against our cheeks and ears.

And the narration continues:

> Letitia was the first to start the game; she was the luckiest and the most privileged of the three of us. Letitia didn't have to dry dishes or make the beds, she could laze away the day reading or pasting up pictures, and at night they let her stay later if she asked to, not counting having a room to herself, special hot bath when she wanted it, and all kinds of other advantages. Little by little she had taken more advantages of these privileges, and had been presiding over

the game since the summer before. I think really she was presiding
over the whole kingdom. (*Blow-Up*, 137–38)

After a while Ariel, a man on the train, throws a message to them
on a small piece of paper. Probably traveling back an forth to an English
school in a Buenos Aires province, he has been watching their statues
and would love to meet them. Hence, next time around he will descend
at the nearest stop. The three girls get immensely excited—Prince
Charming is to greet them and perhaps chose the prettiest among
them. But the excitement soon turns to angst and then hysteria. Letitia
refuses to be at the tracks when Ariel comes, and the other two, nervous, realize he is stupid once they meet him. What's extraordinary is
the way in which the whole experience is narrated as an adolescent
rite of passage—a game of life and death. The girls discover another
dimension to their existence in a trivial playground and with it love,
intrigue, and disappointment.

Humor is also at the core of Cortázar's early short fiction. His literature attempts to be comic, albeit not in a lighthearted way. His esthetic
approach is to intertwine parody and sarcasm, to generate a nervous
smile on the reader's face, and, simultaneously, to make him or her
reflect on a certain mysterious aspect of daily life. Here is a passage
from *Hopscotch*, which allows us to appreciate Cortázar's views of narrative art:

> To attempt the *roman comique* in the sense in which a text manages
> to hint at other values and thus collaborates in that anthropophagy
> that we still consider possible. It would seem that the usual novel
> misses its mark because it limits the reader to its own ambit; the
> better defined it is, the better the novelist is thought to be. An
> unavoidable detention in the varying degrees of the dramatic, the
> psychological, the tragic, the satirical, or the political. To attempt
> on the other hand a text that would not clutch the reader but which
> would oblige him to become an accomplice as it whispers to him
> underneath the conventional exposition other more esoteric direc-
> tions.[36]

Openly humorous or not, Cortázar's stories always hint at other values
and more esoteric directions—they oblige the reader to become an
accomplice, to doubt his or her own certainty. His method, as explained
in "On the Short Story and Its Environs," is based not on falsifying
the mysterious but, instead, on keeping it as true as possible to its

source, with its original tremor, its archetypal stammer. "I realize that when I write a story," he claims in that essay, "I instinctively try to distance myself by means of a demiurge who will live independently, so the reader will have the impression that what he is reading arises somewhat out of himself—with the aid of a *deus ex machina*, to be sure—through the mediation though never the manifest presence of the demiurge." He scrupulously removed himself from any posture that might imply the presence of a moralizing author. His short fiction investigates the exception to the laws of nature, as if the reader, not the author, were in full charge.

Lo Fantástico

The entire discussion of an alternative dimension of things brings me to the second element common in his stories published between 1951 and 1958, from *Bestiary* to *Secret Weapons*: the fantastic—*lo fantástico*. "Almost all the short stories that I have written," he once said, "belong to the genre called 'fantastic' for lack of a better name, and they oppose the false realism that consists in believing that all things can be described and explained according to the philosophical and scientific optimism of the eighteenth century; that is, as part of a world ruled more or less harmoniously by a system of laws or principles, of cause and effect relationships or defined psychologies, of well-mapped geographies" (*Around the Day*, 29). A thorough discussion of the term, widespread in the Hispanic world (think of the Mexican Carlos Fuentes's *Aura*, a 1962 novella Cortázar would have loved to write), was provided by Jaime Alazraki's study *En busca del unicornio*. In the tradition of Roger Caillois, the critic distinguishes between the marvelous and *le fantastique*—mythical, folk, and fairy tales versus supernatural stories. In the former a dreamlike character is introduced to illuminate a moral plot, whereas in the latter an abstract creature is presented to alarm the reader. Furthermore, Alazraki, after discussing Tzvetan Todorov's theories on the subject, which establish a theoretical framework for the fantastic in literary criticism,[37] suggests a difference between the fantastic and the neofantastic. If horror is essential in the first, a sense of perplexity, perhaps even surprise, is achieved in the second without any terrifying ingredient. Thus, Cortázar's *Bestiary*, much like Kafka's oeuvre, belongs to the neofantastic universe.[38] Of his essay "On the Sense of the Fantastic" Cortázar writes, "If the world is not limited to external appearances, it is because the creative spirit of which the poet speaks has metamorphosed the pragmatic functions of memory and the senses: all 'combinatory arts,' the apprehension of subsurface relationships, the sense that all reverses deform, multiply, and annul their obverses are natural for those who *live for the unexpected*" (*Around the Day*, 21–24).

The fantastic was in vogue in Buenos Aires in the 1940s. Borges himself is a most distinguished practitioner. From "The Circular Ruins" to "The Book of Sand," he intertwined reality and fiction in essays and tales. Around 1941, in collaboration with his friends Adolfo Bioy Casares and Sylvina Ocampo, he edited the now-legendary *Antología de literatura fantástica*, translated into English as *The Book of Fantasy*, with a prologue by Ursula Le Guin.[39] Curiously, Borges and Bioy Casares decided not to include Cortázar in their volume. He would finally make it in the second edition of 1965. Although several fellow Argentines had been selected by then (José Bianco, Santiago Dabove, Macedonio Fernández, Leopoldo Lugones, Carlos Peralta, and Manuel Peyrou), and despite Borges's dislike for Cortázar's spontaneous experimentalism, apparently the sheer power of "House Taken Over" made it obligatory to select it as an entry.[40]

Among the stories in *End of the Game* exemplifying Cortázar's interest in the fantastic, "Letter to a Young Lady in Paris," adapted for the screen by Miguel Antín, is about a man in a Buenos Aires apartment on the downtown Suipacha Street, who, hysterically, vomits rabbits. Its genesis, according to Peavler and Picon Garfield, dates back to Cortázar's initiation as a translator. In order to become independent, he needed to pass the exam and thus earn his own money. While preparing for the exams, he began to develop neurotic symptoms, such as recurring nausea. In the story a translator moves into a friend's apartment, as Cortázar himself had done, while she is away in Paris. (Beginning with *Secret Weapons*, the scenario in Cortázar's stories switches, for the most part, from the River Plate to Paris; instead of characters dreaming of France, we get a cast with south American roots—jazz musicians, photographers, artists, cleaning ladies, architects and young professionals—stationed in Europe, whose individual identity is in constant mutation.) He finds that almost every time he rides up in the elevator, between the second and third floor, he vomits a live rabbit, and then doesn't know to hide his shame and the long-eared, short-tailed mammal: "When I feel that I'm going to bring up a rabbit," the text reads, "I put two fingers in my mouth like an open pincer, and I wait to feel the lukewarm fluff rise in my throat like an effervescence in a sal hepatica. It's all swift and clean, passes in a brief instant. I remove the fingers from my mouth and in them, held fast by the ears, is a small white rabbit. The bunny appears to be content, a perfectly normal bunny, only very tiny, small as a chocolate rabbit, only it's white and very thoroughly a rabbit" (*Blow-Up*, 37).

It is vintage Cortázar: sentimentality and melodrama are left out;

the plot is delivered through a first-person narrator, which allows the writer to subjectively confront reality; and despite its absurdity, we feel sympathy toward the situation because the protagonist himself is so overwhelmed by it. A letter written to Andrea, the apartment owner now in Paris, details the place's slow deterioration, the bunnies, reproducing at an incredible rate, overwhelming the entire floor:

> Enough now, I've written this because it's important to me to let you know that I was not all that responsible for the unavoidable and helpless destruction of your home. I'll leave this letter here to you, it would be indecent if the mailman should deliver it some fine clear morning in Paris. Last night I turned the books on the second shelf in the other direction; they were already reaching that high, standing up on their hind legs or jumping, they gnawed off the backs to sharpen their teeth—not that they were hungry, they had all the clover I had bought for them, I store it in the drawers of the writing desk. They tore the curtains, the coverings on the easy chairs, the edge of Augusto Torres' self-portrait, they got fluff all over the rug and besides they tipped, there's no word for it, they stood in a circle under the light of the lamp, in a circle as though they were adoring me, and suddenly they were yipping, they were crying like I never believed rabbits could cry. (*Blow-Up*, 49)

The end, expectedly, is apocalyptic, insinuating the narrator's possible suicide, a favorite Cortázar idea. This type of ending suggests the impossibility of life as it is, the need for something altogether new—a new order, a messianic dimension that will allow our rational universe to expand its scope to other realms of knowledge. Suicide doesn't necessarily mean death in the tragic sense but in the humorous one: in Cortázar's view, our modern-day neurosis pushes us to the very limit of our existence, to extremes that force us to reevaluate our entire approach to routine. A similar suicidal end appears in one of his most anthologized pieces, "Don't You Blame Anyone," an extraordinary one-paragraph-long tale in which an anonymous man unsuccessfully tries to put on a sweater—until, desperate and fatalistic, he throws himself out the window. Here is Alberto Manguel's translation:

> maybe he has fallen to his knees and he feels as if suspended by his left hand tugging once again at the sweater and suddenly it's cold on his eyebrows and forehead, on the eyes, absurdly he doesn't want to open his eyes but he knows he's out, that cold substance,

that delightful substance is the open air, and he doesn't want to open his eyes and he waits one second, two seconds, he allows himself to live in a cold and different time, the time of outside the sweater, he's on his knees and it's beautiful to be like that, until little by little he gratefully opens his eyes freed from the blue spider's web of wool inside, he opens his eyes carefully and sees the five black fingernails hovering over his eyes, and he has just enough time to lower his eyelids and throw himself back, covering himself with the left hand which is his hand, that is all he has left to defend him from inside the sleeve, to pull at the sweater's collar upwards, and the blue web is spun around his face once more, while he picks himself up to run away some place else, to reach at least some place without the hand, without the sweater, some place where there is only fragrant air to envelop him and accompany him and caress him and twelve floors down.[41]

In Cortázar's hands, the normal act of putting on a sweater turns into an epic challenge. He isn't offering a pragmatic, utilitarian portrait; instead, his ojective is to explore the domestic realm to show how, beyond its tranquil surface, it is made up of labyrinthine, chaotic paths. Death, in the end of the story, is not invoked to create a feeling of sadness; it brings laughter, because most readers can identify with the struggle to find one's way through a complicated piece of clothing.

Inspired by a 1952 accident Cortázar suffered while riding a Vespa in France, "The Night Face Up" is about a twentieth-century man convalescing from a similar accident who has nightmares about a pre-Columbian Indian fleeing the Aztecs. The transtemporal connection between the two is taken to its ultimate limits. The Aztecs are pursuing the Indian because they need sacrificial victims. And just as he is about to be killed at the top of a pyramid, he projects his dreams to the future. The torches around him become traffic lights. He suffers a metamorphosis and becomes the man astride the motorcycle. "He managed to close his eyelids again, although he knew now he was not going to wake up," writes Cortázar, "that he was awake, that the marvelous dream had been the other absurd as all dreams are" (*Blow-Up*, 66). Cortázar establishes a bridge and a sense of continuity between past and present. The story's underlying thesis is unquestionably Borgesian: nothing in a person's life is truly original; every life is an endless chain of repetitions that have populated humankind since the beginning. It also seems to suggest that links between people are not always apparent; they are hidden, implicit, mystical. A similar thesis, about doubles and transmigration of souls, about bridges uniting different worlds, "Axolotl" centers on a man living in Paris who visits an aquarium and becomes so engrossed with a Mexican salamander that he penetrates the glass and merges physically with the body of the amphibian.[42] He peers through the glass for hours while the watchman uncomfortably witnesses. While he remains trapped, he relates the story. The entire text is narrated in the first person, with the sole exception of the last paragraph, stressing the interchanging of identities:

> He returned many times, but he comes less often now. Weeks pass without his showing up. I saw him yesterday, he looked at me for a long time and left briskly. It seemed to me that he was not so much interested in us any more, that he was coming out of habit. Since the only thing I do is think, I could think about him a lot. It occurs to me that he felt more than ever one with the mystery which was claiming him. But the bridges were broken between him and me, because what was his obsession is now an axolotl, alien to his human life. I think that at the beginning I was capable of returning to him in a certain way—ah, only in a certain way—and of keeping awake his desire to know us better I am an axolotl for good now, and if I think like a man it's only because every axolotl thinks like a man inside his rosy stone semblance I believe that all this succeeded in communicating something to him in those first days, when I was still he. And in this final solitude to which he now longer comes, I console myself by thinking that perhaps he is going to write a story about us, that, believing he's making a story, he's going to write all this about axolotls. (*Blow-Up*, 9)

Shifting viewpoints and creating bridges between different realities is a permanent theme in Cortázar's short fiction. A most challenging story, probably his most ambitious, "Blow-Up," adapted for the screen in 1966 by director Michelangelo Antonioni (which expanded Cortázar's international reputation immensely),[43] is about many things at once, including a document on photography as an art and weapon, a study of morality in today's society, and an experiment with multiple ways of retelling a plot. As translated by the American poet Paul Blackburn, its beginning is legendary: "It'll never be known how this has to be told, in the first person or in the second, using the third person plural or continually inventing modes that will serve for nothing. If one might say: I will see the moon rose, or: we hurt me at the back of my eyes, and especially: you the blond woman was the clouds that race beyond my your his our yours their face, What the hell!" (*Blow-Up*, 114).[44] Cortázar not only experiments with content here but also with form: he breaks language apart, renews its syntax, and pushes its grammar to the limit. Indeed, the story's language is as much a protagonist as Roberto Michel, a translator and photography aficionado of French and Chilean background, and the voice through which we attempt to witness an elusive action. Calling him the protagonist might thus be an error, since according to Nicolás Bratosevich, the true leading character in "Blow-Up" is Time, with a capital "T." Or, as Flora Schiminovich suggests, it is death (although the second paragraph announces Michel's death—"One of us all has to write, if this is going to be told. Better that it be me who am dead" [*Blow-Up*, 115]—it is never clear when and how he died).[45] Or, better perhaps, it's the camera lens (Contax I.I.2), which becomes the voice and conscience of the text, insinuating a future action that is difficult to know.[46] Some critics have even suggested it is the passing clouds that narrate the events, which signals the endless interpreting debate that surrounds the story since it was first published in 1958. But Gordana Yovanovich thinks otherwise: she believes the protagonist to be the story's reader: "the story has meaning only if it means something to readers" (Yovanovich, 194). Whatever we settle for, "Blow-Up" is an exploration of narrative perspectives and social morality.

Critics tend to examine the story in moral terms and have suggested that Michel's identity and his sanity are destroyed by the imaginative reliving of experience; this means that he is driven insane and cracks up. As Cortázar keeps on reminding the reader, the enigma at the core of his story "will never be known" (114). Since the verbal tense is continuously shifting from present to past to future, from "I" to "he," linguistic experimentation, progress, and regression are the textual leitmotivs. Cortázar's story, set in Paris, on Ile-Saint-Louis—as in "The Island at Noon," wherein a transforming event occurs away from urban dwellings—is about Michel, who lives on the fifth floor of 11 Rue Monsieur-le-Prince, wandering around an island where, by pure chance, he witnesses a possible crime.

A couple who look like a mother and her child are alone. Are they related? Secret lovers? Parners in an illicit action? Michel shoots some pictures and is ready to leave when the man with the gray hat comes toward him and asks him to return them. The photographer claims he is free to take any photo he wants and leaves. Shortly thereafter, on a Sunday afternoon, he develops the roll, enlarges a few pictures, and, after carefully studying the snapshots, discovers a man with a gray hat sitting in a car, at some distance, observing the action. Is there a link between the boy and the man in the car? Michel comes to believe a homosexual liaison between the male characters was forthcoming; the woman, a prostitute, functions as their intermediary.[47] The amateur photographs in Michel's studio soon acquire a life of their own, and while the conclusion is open to interpretation, the characters in the pictures contribute to his device—one to be introduced again in the political story "Apocalypse in Solentiname."

Another theme in "Blow-Up," the nervous shifting of narrative perspectives, can be further understood by analyzing "Señorita Cora." Less complicated and considerably more accessible, the story deals with a surgical operation performed in a Buenos Aires hospital on a teenager, Pablo, also called El Nene. When one of the nurses on duty, Miss Cora, takes his temperature rectally, he becomes nervous and sexually excited. Unexpectedly, the operation goes wrong and the nurse, at the patient's side, becomes attached to him, her preliminary coldness shifting to warmth and even love. In the same paragraph Cortázar intertwines the boy's stream of consciousness and dialogue, his mother's, Miss Cora's, as well as the intern Marcial's. The result is a Rashomon-like story where a sum of voices acquires a symphonic tone.

A favorite Cortázar theme unifying many of the stories written until 1959 is the quest—*una pesquisa*, a pursuit for another reality, a better life. "The Pursuer," a longer text critics describe as a novella, is, according to Sosnowski, Alazraki, Susana Jakfalvi, Ferré, and other critics, the turning point in Cortázar's career, the door leading to *Hopscotch* and future novels. Inspired by the life and music of the alto saxophonist Charlie Parker,[48] the narrative tells of the impossible desire by Bruno, his biographer, to capture the essence of Johnny Carter's evanescent existence, his journey into drugs, alcohol, and despair.[49] The dualities of the human condition are keenly exposed in this much-analyzed story. The reader is asked to recognize the individual nature of things and, as usual in Cortázar, to look for a higher meaning. The Argentine's two characters are built as Manichean mirrors; they symbolize sanity and lunacy, coherence and incoherence, and that invites a comparison between them and Cervantes's Don Quixote and Sancho Panza: while Carter is a romantic idealist, a dreamer in constant search of perfection and the sublime, Bruno is an ambitious materialist who understands that the more suffering Carter undergoes, the most appealing his biography will be.[50] In fact, the character of the pursuer can be found at every corner of Cortázar's short and long fiction. "If in fact Johnny's quest can really arouse our emotions," says Sosnowski, "can induce us to empathize with him to the point of identifying ourselves with what he does not quite manage to say, it is Bruno who stirs up all these reactions through his narration, through his confession in the eyes of Johnny's challenge. Johnny's biography, as transmitted through the omissions he himself and Bruno make, is a mask, a false face for the consumer."[51] As Picon Garfield states, "The Pursuer" was written almost by a miracle of fate. Cortázar was searching for a protagonist for a short story that would not be fantastic, when he read the obituary of Charlie Parker in a Paris newspaper.

After writing the first episode, he had a mental block and could not continue. Months later, while in Geneva on business for UNESCO, he found the papers in a briefcase, reread them, and began work again. In two days he had finished writing one of his most successful works. "I realized several years later that if I hadn't written 'The Pursuer,' I would have been incapable of writing *Hopscotch*," he said (quoted in Garfield 1975, 46–47). Cortázar's story is often read alongside another one by one his contemporaries, the African-American writer James Baldwin, whose 1957 story "Sonny's Blues" (included in the collection *Going to Meet the Man*) is about jazz in Harlem. In it two brothers, a successful schoolteacher and a drug addict, find each other when the former accepts the artistic quest of the latter, his younger sibling. Together, Cortázar and Baldwin offer a complementary portrait of the black music world. In Cortázar's text, Johnny Carter is an expatriate unable to deal with America; in Baldwin's, Sonny is exiled at home—a victim of his own destructive milieu and temperament.

Two years after his arrival in Paris, Cortázar married Aurora Bernárdez, another Argentine translator, a very bright and educated woman with whom he visited Italy and Greece, where he began developing his characters Cronopios and Fames. In a memoir published in the Mexican magazine *Vuelta* and later used as the preface to Cortázar's *Complete Stories*, Mario Vargas Llosa recalls meeting the couple:

> I met them . . . [in 1958] in the house of a common friend, in Paris, and since then, until the last time I saw them together, in 1967, in Greece—where the three of us were translators in an international conference on cotton—I never stopped being astonished by the spectacle of listening to their dialogue *ad tandem*. Everybody else

looked like an uninvited guest. Everything they said was intelligent, sophisticated, enjoyable, vital. I thought many times: "They can't be always like this. They must rehearse these type of conversations, at home, in order to impress the listeners with unexpected anecdotes, brilliant quotes and jokes that, at the correct moment, loosen up the atmosphere a little bit." . . . It is hard to determine who had read more and better and which of the two offered more acute comments on books and writers. The fact that Julio wrote and Aurora *only* translated (in her case the word *only* means something altogether different to its normal connotation) was something I supposed to be provisional, Aurora's transitory sacrifice so that in the family there would only be one writer.[52]

A short while later, around 1968, Cortázar and Bernárdez separated. Vargas Llosa, whose early titles *The Green House* and *Conversation in the Cathedral* Cortázar admired a great deal, concludes:

> we would spend the morning together [in Greece] and in the afternoon we would participate in the translation conference, in a room at the Hilton, and at night in Plaka restaurants, near the Acropolis, where we would always have dinner. Together we visited museums, orthodox churches, temples, and in a weekend, the island of Hydra. When I returned to London, I told [my wife,] Patricia: "The perfect couple exists. Aurora and Julio have managed to perform a miracle: they have a happy marriage." A few days later Julio wrote to me announcing their separation. I have never felt more disoriented. (*Cuentos completos*, 13–14)

Politics and the Story

After 1958 Cortázar, his reputation still limited to a circle of initiated few, made a fundamental artistic shift; he abandoned the short fiction genre and (again) devoted himself to the novel. *The Winners* (1960) was his first one published. He thought he needed to explore new narrative horizons, and "The Pursuer" was proof of a desire to expand and be inclusive. After visits to the United States, mainly Washington, D.C., and New York,[53] he devoted himself to a transitional work: *Cronopios and Fames* (1962), playful pseudo-essays now almost totally forgotten. Having finished the section on Cronopios, at first mimeographed as a private edition and distributed to friends, someone suggested he expand certain sections, and thus the volume was born. When the book was published the reaction, unlike the applause that had greeted *End of the Game* and *Secret Weapons*, was negative. While poets loved it, critics attacked it for its lack of serious intentions, as if the novelist had abandoned his style and themes for sheer frivolity. Lacking unity, the volume, written between 1952 and 1959, in Italy, France, and Argentina, is, in Cortázar's words, "really a game, a fascinating game, very amusing: . . . almost like a tennis match. There were no serious intentions" (quoted in Garfield 1975, 50). Cortázar's fame became international when *Hopscotch* was published in 1963. Alongside García Márquez's *One Hundred Years of Solitude* (1967), many critics consider it one of the premier Latin American literary works of the twentieth century.

In 1966 Cortázar visited Cuba for the first time. Since 1958, Fidel Castro had become a regional idol, and Spanish-speaking intellectuals, after Castro's invitation to "see the island for themselves," considered their role crucial in reeducating the masses along the road to socialism. Cortázar fell under the tyrant's spell and became an active supporter of the revolution. Although he had been involved in Argentine politics in his adolescence, this no doubt was a reversal of considerable importance. As stated, in his early creative period (1945–66) he had ignored social causes. When critics suggested ideological readings to his work, he quickly rejected their interpretations. But this attitude changed in

Part 1

the 1960s. According to Eduardo Galeano's trilogy *Memory of Fire*, Cortázar, at least politically speaking, "went from the end toward the beginning; from discouragement to enthusiasm, from indifference to passion, from solitude to solidarity."[54] In a 10 May 1967 letter to his friend the Cuban intellectual Roberto Fernández Retamar, editor of the cultural magazine *Casa de las Américas*, Cortázar wrote,

> At times I wonder what my work would have been like if I had remained in Argentina; I know that I would have continued writing because I'm not good at anything else, but judging by what I had done by the time I left my country, I am inclined to believe that I would have continued along the crowded thoroughfare of intellectual escapism I had traveled until then and which is still the path of a great many Argentine intellectuals of my generation and my taste. If I had to enumerate the causes for which I am glad I left my country (and let it be very clear that I am only speaking for myself as an individual and not as any sort of model), I believe the main one would be the Cuban revolution. For me to become convinced of this it's enough to talk from time to time with Argentine friends who pass through Paris evincing the saddest ignorance of what is really happening in Cuba; all I have to do is glance at the newspapers read by twenty million of my compatriots: that's enough to make me feel protected here from the influence that is wielded by U.S. information in my country and which an infinite number of Argentine writers and artists of my generation do not escape, even though they sincerely think they do; every day they are stirred by the subliminal mill wheels of United Press and "democratic" magazines that march to the tune of *Time* and *Life*.[55]

In essays and lectures he began to support the idea that, while involved in social and political issues, the writer needs to be left alone to write literature. He recognized his intellectual responsibility toward the future of humankind, and yet he advocated artistic freedom and was against the Communist concept of socialist realism, an esthetic approach to art that had silenced many top Soviet and Eastern European writers, such as Isaac Babel, the author of *Odessa Stories* and *Red Chivalry*, during and after World War II.[56] In 1969 Cortázar participated in a controversial debate with Vargas Llosa and Oscar Collazos, in which the latter, in the Uruguayan magazine *Marcha*, attacked the Latin American Boom writers as derivative, ideologically inconsequential, and sold to the establishment. Cortázar responded ferociously in an essay entitled "Literature in Revolution and Revolution in Literature," in which his views of socialist realism and his attitude toward a revolutionary art became even clearer as he denounced those on the Left who failed to reach a consciousness that "is much more revolutionary than the revolutionaries tend to have."[57] In a debate preposterous in today's perspective, Cortázar kept on defending the revolutionary nature of his books. And shortly thereafter, when the Heberto Padilla affair exploded in 1971,[58] he joined a number of Latin American writers who signed a letter of protest.

Nevertheless, Cortázar, unlike Octavio Paz and Vargas Llosa, refused to turn his back on the Cuban regime when the affair became acrimonious. His stand put him in a difficult position: he was in favor of artistic freedom but backed a government that jailed a poet for his writings and later[59] forced the prisoner to openly denounce himself as counterrevolutionary after what was clearly a brainwashing and torture session. Cortázar's deepest political transformation took place in May 1968, when the student uprising hit Paris while civic upheaval shook Mexico's Tlatelolco Square and Prague's Spring erupted. Suddenly he found himself participating in barricades, handing out flyers denouncing the establishment, and talking about "the imagination of power." When Cortázar died, Octavio Paz wrote a touching obituary in his literary magazine *Vuelta*:

> He was a cornerstone of contemporary Latin American letters. He had my age. Although he lives in Buenos Aires and I in Mexico, I met him early on, in 1945; the two of us contributed to *Sur*, and thanks to José Bianco, we soon began exchanging correspondence and books. Years later we coincided in Paris and for a while we saw each other frequently. Later on, I abandoned Europe, lived in the Far East and returned to Mexico. My relationship with Julio was not interrupted. In 1968 he and Aurora Bernárdez lived with me and [my wife] Marie José in our house in New Delhi. It was around that time that Julio discovered politics, and he embraced with fervor and naïveté causes that also ignited me in the past but that, at that point, I already judged reproachable. I ceased to see him, but not to love him. I think he also kept considering me a friend. Through the barriers of paper and words, we made each other friendly signs.[60]

In 1966 Cortázar published his fifth and probably best second-epoch collection of stories, *All Fires the Fire*, containing eight entries. Among the most memorable entries included is "Instructions for John Howell," unique in its use of prose to penetrate the secrets of theater. Dedicated to Peter Brook, the British director and author of *The Open Space*,[61] it is about a spectator at a play who, in the intermission after act 1, is called by two anonymous men to go backstage, where he is suddenly given instructions to replace one of the leading actors. He first refuses and then concedes. Once on stage he improvises and, much to his surprise, his performance fits perfectly the rhythm of the rest of the cast. Things turn chaotic. After act 2 he is not only thrown off the stage but out the theater, and another member of the audience replaces him.

Cortázar's story ought to be read alongside two other tales by recognized Latin American masters also dealing with the stage: Borges's "Averroes's Search"[62] and Juan Carlos Onetti's "A Dream Fulfilled."[63] In the former, the medieval Muslim philosopher, while writing an exegetical commentary on Aristotle's *Poetics*, tries in vain to understand the meaning of the terms *comedy* and *tragedy*. Because of a religious dictum, theaters are forbidden in his immediate milieu. He therefore needs to explain the concept of comedy without ever having seen a stage, so Averroes comes up with a totally absurd definition.[64] Onetti's take, on the other hand, is more like Cortázar's: Langman, a second-rate producer in a province of Uruguay, far from Buenos Aires, the theater capital of South America, is hired by a young and beautiful woman to re-create a dream she had in which, for the first time in her life, she was truly happy. Langman puts together a small cast, and the young lady asks to be part of it. When the one-performance-only play takes place, the actress dies at the climatic moment, reality having been too difficult for her to handle. She needed to re-create a dream to return to Paradise—only to then vanish.[65] While Onetti's tale is existential, "Instructions for John Howell" suggest the universe as a Pirandellian forum—reality is a stage and every human an improvisational actor. And, echoing Borges, in a tribute to Artaud's "Theater of Cruelty," Lee Strasberg's "Living Theater," and other revolutionary institutions of the 1960s, Cortázar insinuates that theater is a pure Western creation, a labyrinth where emotions run high, a microcosm of the Western psyche.

During the 1970s Cortázar, in esthetic terms, explored what I call the art of literary promiscuity. After *All Fires the Fire* he published two playful, amorphous texts, called "collage books": *Around the Day in Eighty Worlds* and *Last Round*. In between he published *62: A Model Kit*, a sequel to *Hopscotch*, published in 1968 in Buenos Aires by Editorial

Sudamericana, about vampires and city landscapes, a theme he began exploring in *La otra orilla*. Perhaps the best example of this period is the literary promiscuity in which he engaged. Using traditional genres was not enough any more; he needed to surmount barriers, to write prose poems, essayist stories, nonfiction novels—to intertwine separate structures, imposing chaos. An example of this avant-garde miscegenation is his essay "A Country Called Alechinsky," a tribute to an Argentine painter and friend, Alechinsky. He chooses to write about him from the perspective of ants crawling across his drawings and paintings at night, how they perceive the world, what they think and concoct. Neither a story nor a nonfiction piece, the text is a hybrid. "He doesn't known we like to roam through his paintings," it begins in Thomas Christensen's translation, "that we have long loved to adventure through his drawings and engravings, examining each twist and each labyrinth with a secret attention, with an endless palpation of antennae."[66] As it develops, the information, the reader realizes, is factual, but its shape belongs to descriptions often found in fiction. The explicit purpose is to confuse: to mix tradition, to intertwine expository and creative writing. When compared with other Latin American writers, I should say, Cortázar was just developing a trend: Borges had already redefined the borderline where the essay and the short story confront each other; and Paz, in *The Children of Mire* (1974) and *The Philantropic Ogre* (1979), had restructured the essay to become more discursive and exegetical, but also more poetic.

This nonconventional drive went even further. In 1975 came another rare experiment: *Fantomas vs. the Multinational Vampires*, a now out-of-print "socialist" comic strip that used a famous dime novel character placed in an ideological war against aggressive capitalist forces. Just before Cortázar put together his second poetry collection, *Pameos and meopas* (1971), and published what, according to Ferré, is his most important work, *Observatory Prose* (1972), a volume of illustrated essays, he wrote another novel, *A Manual for Manuel* (1972), his most politically outspoken to date. He also traveled to Argentina, with short visits to Peru, Ecuador, and Chile; lectured at the University of Oklahoma; participated in the PEN-sponsored Translation Conference in New York City; and wrote an important introduction to Felisberto Hernández's *The Flooded House and Other Stories* and assessments of Horacio Quiroga and Roberto Arlt.[67] Indeed, it was obvious at this point in his career that, aside from Borges, Hernández, Arlt, and Horacio Quiroga had greatly influenced Cortázar's short stories. Over the decades, in

Hernández, whom Cortázar first read in his thirties, he had found inspiration for stories such as "House Taken Over" and "End of the Game," which resemble "The Flooded House" and "The Daisy Dolls." (Curiously, Hernández and Cortázar lived in Chivilcoy at the same time, in 1939, but apparently they never met.) He got from him the capacity to find "the most subtle relationship between things, that eyeless dance of the most ancient elements; untouchable smoke and fire; the high cupola of a cloud on the random message of a simple herb; evrything that is marvelous and obscure in the world" (*Obra crítica*, 3: 269; my translation).

Cortázar had read Arlt in his twenties. He had admired his "styleless" and chaotic street language, his "weak" prose, and the urgency and anarchy of his plots. He found him to be a great writer who looked for knowledge through the avalanche of darkness and his own artistic power in his infinite weakness (*Obra crítica*, 3: 260). And in Quiroga he had found the raw explorer of the South American jungle, both in the concrete and the imaginary sense, the writer as muscle man, à la Hemingway—the pathfinder, the pioneer, the trailblazer who would penetrate inhospitable habitats and return to write a magical story about man's struggle with nature. A decade before his death, Cortázar, through evocative essays and introductions, established genealogical lines between him and those he recognized as his precursors, making sure his oeuvre would be appreciated in the correct literary tradition.

His political commitment was at its peak in the late 1970s. He had donated the money of the Prix Médicis to the United Chilean Front. His liberalism was in sharp contrast with Borges, who was spending his mature life articulating a right-wing, semi-fascist position in which the artist is glorified sub specie aeternitatis. Between 1974 and 1983 Cortázar returned to the short fiction genre to write four more collections: *Octaedro* (1974), with seven entries; *Someone Walking Around* (1977), with eleven; *We Love Glenda So Much* (1981), with ten; and *Bad Timing* (1983), with eight. He took some breaks: for instance, in 1978 he published *Territories* and in 1979 his last novel, *A Certain Lucas*, a philosophical investigation into the daily activities of a common man, which is strikingly similar to Calvino's *Mr. Palomar*.

"Politics in a work of literature," wrote Stendhal, "is like a pistol-shot in the middle of a concert, something loud and vulgar, and yet a thing to which it is not possible to refuse one's attention."[68] In the case of Cortázar, the pistol shot is apparent in a handful of tales, written as he reassessed his oeuvre in intellectual terms. Set in the 1970s,

"Press Clippings" is about a female Argentine writer in Paris asked by a sculptor of the Rue Riquet to write a text for his exhibition catalog about torture in the Third World. She receives from him an envelop with a number of newspaper clippings detailing the unspeakable tragedy of a Jewish woman exiled in Mexico, whose husband, daughter, and other relatives were killed or are among the *desaparecidos* of the Buenos Aires military junta. The first one, which Cortázar quotes verbatim from an Argentine newspaper, read as follows:

> The undersigned, Laura Beatriz Bonaparte Bruschtein, domiciled at no. 26 Atoyac, District 10, Colonia Cuauthémoc, Mexico 5, D.F., wishes to pass the following testimony on the public opinion:
>
> 1. Aída Leonora Bruschtein Bonaparte, born May 21, 1951, in Buenos Aires, Argentina, profession, teacher in literacy program.
>
> *Fact*: At ten o'clock in the morning of December 24, 1975, she was kidnapped by personnel of the Argentine army (601st Battalion) at her place of employment in the Monte Chingolo slum, near the federal capital.
>
> The previous day that place had been the scene of a battle that had left a toll of one hundred dead, including habitants of the area. My daughter, after being kidnapped, was taken to the military headquarters of the 601st Battalion.
>
> There she was brutally murdered, the same as other women. Those who survived were shot the same Christmas night. Among them was my daughter.
>
> The burial of those killed in the fighting and of the civilians kidnapped, as was the case of my daughter, was delayed for about five days. All the bodies, including hers, were transferred in mechanical shovels from the battalion to the Lanús police station where they were buried in a common grave. (*We Love Glenda So Much*, 83–84)

What follows is a juxtaposition of the Paris writer's discovery of Laura Beatriz Bonaparte Bruschtein's ordeal and her doubts regarding the role of artists and writers in society—particularly during the so-called dirty war in Argentina, when many left-wing supporters were tortured and killed. Indeed, Cortázar's story, a call to artists to be active in the opposition to dictatorial governments (Cuba excluded), ought to be read as an illustration of Antonio Gramsci's concept of organic intellectuals, never isolated and passive, always involved in a process of active transformation.

In the second part of "Press Clippings" a reversal takes place, as the female narrator is forced to confront a violent dilemma in her own neighborhood. As she returns from the sculptor's house, she sees a crying young girl sitting on her doorstep. When asked why she is suffering, the girl answers: "My mama. . . . My papa is doing things to my mama" (*We Love Glenda So Much*, 90). Lead by her, the writer enters a miserable apartment to witnesses a man keeping a woman tied up to a bed, slowly burning her breast and skin near her vagina. Outraged, she hits the man with a chair. But as expected in Cortázar's oeuvre, in newspaper accounts read days later, the mother tied up on the bed was also a torturer who eventually kills her husband. The political message is crystal clear: in a state of war, nobody is innocent; ideology tarnishes all aspects of the world, and one person's report is always partial and subjective.

"Apocalypse in Solentiname," reprinted, with a sequel, in *Nicaraguan Sketches* (1984),[69] is one of Cortázar's most celebrated political tales. It concerns Ernesto Cardenal, a Nicaraguan poet and Nicaragua's minister of culture during the Sandinista regime of Daniel Ortega. After studying at Columbia University and already ordained as a Catholic priest, Cardenal in 1966 began building a religious community among the campesinos and fishermen in Solentiname, an archipelago at the southern tip of Lake Nicaragua, near Costa Rica. Cortázar's story is based on a 1977 attack, killing many, by Somoza's National Guard.[70] It is a straightforward, first-person account of a trip to Costa Rica, where the protagonist, an Argentine writer, in what appears to be a book tour, meets his friends Carmen Naranjo,[71] Samuel Rovinski,[72] Sergio Ramírez,[73] and later on Cardenal himself.

After a chat and some interviews, he is flown to Solentiname, where he parties, meets people, and, when ready to go to sleep, sees a bunch of beautiful paintings in a corner. "I don't remember who explained to me that they were the work of peasants from the region," he writes. "This one was painted by Vicente, this is by Ramona, some signed and others not, but all so beautiful, once more the first version of the world, the clean look of a person who describes what's around him like a song of praise: midget cows in poppy fields, the sugar-making shed with people coming out like ants, the horse with green eyes against the background of cane fields, a baptism in a church that doesn't believe in perspective and climbs up or falls down on top of itself, the lake with little boats like shoes and in the background an enormous fish laughing with turquoise teeth" (*A Change of Light*, 121–22).

Like Roberto Michel in "Blow-Up," Cortázar secretly gets his camera out and takes photographs of each of the paintings, after which he tells Cardenal about his discovery and how he froze the images. "Art thief," the Nicaraguan poet answers, "image smuggler" (123). The sale of the paintings, the Argentine soon finds out, helped improve the town's social condition. The voyage to Solentiname and back ends happily. Cortázar then travels to Havana and home to Paris. Months later his girlfriend, Claudine, develops the film, including of a number of snapshots of other landscapes as well, and when the Argentine, at home alone, sees the slides, he is astonished. Instead of a scene reminiscent of the beautiful paintings by peasants, he sees a massacre by Nicaraguan soldiers and the death of Roque Dalton, the Salvadoran poet and revolutionary repeatedly imprisoned for political activities, who lived exiled in Cuba and Czechoslovakia and was assassinated by a rival leftist faction in 1975:[74]

> I saw a clearing in the jungle, a cabin with a thatched roof and trees in the foreground, against the trunk of the nearest one a thin fellow looking to the left where a confused group, five or six of them close together, were aiming rifles and pistols at him; the fellow with a long face and a lock of hair falling down over his dark forehead was looking at them, one hand half-raised, the other probably in his pants pockets, it was as if he were saying something to them unhurriedly, almost listlessly, and even through the photograph was hazy I sensed and I knew that the fellow was Roque Dalton, and then I did press the button as if with that I could save him from the infamy of that death. (*A Change of Light*, 125–26)

Sometime later, Claudine returns home and looks at the photographs on her own. She, in a vintage Cortazarian reversal, sees only the beautiful campesino paintings. As in "The Island at Noon," readers are thus encouraged to believe the protagonist and narrator had a vision—a prophetic sight of a tragic future. The text recalls the fashion in which poor Chilean women after 1973, when Pinochet's coup d'état ended the Salvador Allende presidency, created *arpilleras*, colorful quilts in which they embroidered political messages denouncing the dictatorship and requesting information about *desaparecido* family members. These *arpilleras* would be smuggled out of the country, communicating to the outside world the atrocities silenced by the military junta. In Cortázar's eyes, an apparently neutral artifact of folklore is perceived as a testament of the people's suffering; what's needed is a new way to understand its hidden message.

His obsession with political struggle is even more obvious in a less successful, openly historical tale, "Reunion," about the plight of Fidel Castro and Ernesto "Ché" Guevara in the Sierra Maestra. "I tried to fit in 20 pages," Cortázar said in an interview with Omar Prego, "all the essence, the engine, the revolutionary spirit that led the bearded guerrilleros to power. . . . [T]he story marked my entrance in the political or ideological conscience."[75] The event described is the origin of the Cuban Revolution—the moment, on 6 December 1956, when a group of 82 rebels under Castro's command, comming from Mexico, where they had trained for a few months after the Moncada defeat, disembarked in Oriente province, in Cuba's southern section. The revolutionaries find Batista's army is awaiting them. They then divide in two groups: Fidel and one bunch go to Alegría del Río, where they stay for three days, and then proceed to the Sierra Maestra, where they find the other group, led by Raúl Castro and Ché Guevara. The story deals with the events happening to Ché's faction until they find Castro (called Luis in the text) in the Sierra Maestra, and the suspense is built on the fighters not knowing if Fidel is alive. In this tale Cortázar puts literature at the service of ideology, and thus his characters are flat, cartoonlike. They fail to inspire sympathy or pity in us; they are superficial, puppets used to deliver a political message. "Reunion" testifies to the Argentine's strong commitment to the Communist regime in Havana. At a time, in the late 1960s, when other Latin American and Spanish intellectuals such as Octavio Paz, Juan Goytisolo, and Vargas Llosa began to distance themselves from the Cuban regime, Cortázar, more stubborn and apparently less flexible, showed, through his writing, his devotion to Castro's dream.

Utopianism south of the Rio Grande and the hardships of the modern, mechanical world possessed Cortázar day in and day out. The inspiration for Jean-Luc Godard's film *Weekend* (1967), "Southern Thruway" studies the human tolerance to traffic jams. During a typical Sunday afternoon, the thousands of commuters who return to Paris by car find themselves stuck in the middle of the highway. Nobody moves for minutes, then hours, days, and even weeks. After a while characters begin to develop relationships and find a way to adapt to the extreme situation. Small groups begin to administer security and food. Station wagons become ambulances, and trucks keep the dead. A new status quo is established, and when finally things get moving, the new, improvised society is dissolved to everybody's sadness. Nobody believes that tomorrow they will be back at their regular Paris jobs and a male character will never see the child he just conceived, nor the woman to whom he made love, since they did not exchange addresses. Cortázar's text is a comment on modern technology and human adaptability and a critique of our impersonal means of communication and transportation. His characters are victims of circumstance, prisoners of progress. He examines the laws of determinism while, indirectly, suggesting the need for a new human equilibrium. Three decades after its initial composition, with the never-ending deterioration of urban traffic and its ubiquitous presence in television images, the plot of "Southern Thruway" has become a commonplace, making it look a bit outdated. But its sheer existence, at the same time, makes Cortázar a visionary of sorts; he was exploring the artistic potential of urban apocalypses at a time when people were still fighting against robotlike behavior imposed by modern technology.

My favorite Cortázar story of the second creative period (1967–83) is "We Love Glenda So Much," a high-caliber study of mass media's impact on society and the infatuation of film viewers. A group of devoted fans of the actress Glenda Jackson—Glenda Garson in Cortázar's tale—become a camaraderie after a few members find themselves attending the same movies: *Snow Fire, The Uses of Elegance,* and *Fragile Returns.* "In those days it was hard to know," says the narrator:

> You go to the movies or the theater and live your night without thinking about the people who have already gone through the same ceremony, choosing the place and time, getting dressed and telephoning and row eleven or five, the darkness and the music, territory that belongs to nobody and to everybody there where everybody is nobody, the men or women in their seats, maybe a word of apology for arriving late, a murmur comment that someone picks up or ignores, almost always silence, looks pouring onto the stage or the screen, fleeing from what's beside them, from what's on this side. (*We Love Glenda So Much,* 8)

As in Woody Allen's *The Purple Rose of Cairo* (1985), Cortázar investigates that borderline between each side of the screen. The fans go to special screenings and become enchanted with their idol in such a way that, when Glenda makes a new movie and they find it imperfect, they tacitly decide to kidnap every single copy available, in all corners of the world, and correct, through a masterful technological device, the film's errors: "The most difficult part was, of course, deciding on the changes, the cuts, the modifications in montage and rhythm; our different ways of feeling Glenda brought on harsh confrontations that calmed down only after long analyses and in some cases the imposition of majority rule in the nucleus" (*We Love Glenda So Much*, 13). After a while the group feels tempted to go beyond—not only to correct Glenda's last film but the little imperfections in every one she ever made. And they succeed. Nobody finds out that the old copies have been improved—and when anybody does, an article appears in a newspaper, a little scandal emerges without real consequences. Soon enough and to the group's fortune, Glenda announces her retirement, which means they have emerged victorious: their version of the actress's filmography will remain intact, there will be no new additions to her canon. Expectedly, things turn bad when Glenda, changing her mind, decides to give up her retirement and make more movies. The only solution is to assassinate her, to retain her presence on the silver screen by destroying her real persona. Cortázar's comment is unambiguous: it is not Glenda but Glenda's image that truly counts—not the self but its appearance: "We separated, undone, already living what would happen on a day that only one of us would know ahead of time. We were sure we wouldn't meet again at the café, that each of us from then on would hide the solitary perfection of our realm" (*We Love Glenda So Much*, 16).

It would be a mistake to suggest that in the late 1960s Cortázar's literary obsessions were uniformly injected with a doses of ideology; in fact, his second creative period also includes nonpolitical tales. "A Change of Light" details the relationship between Tito Balcárcel, a radio soap-opera actor, and Luciana, a female fan who writes him an admiring letter. A bit shy, Tito responds, beginning an affair that ultimately fails because of the expectations the two had about the other. Early on, before knowing Luciana, Tito visualizes who she is, and she does a similar thing about him. But reality and expectations never match, and at the end their relationship fails while he sees her coming out of a hotel with another Tito, one fitting her expectations:

> Tell her, perhaps. I didn't have time, I think I hesitated because I preferred keeping her like that, the fulfillment was so great that I didn't want to think about her vague silence, a distraction I hadn't known in her before, a way of looking at me for moments as if searching, something, quiver of a glance returned immediately to

the immediate, to the cat or to a book. That, too, entered into my way of preferring her, it was the melancholy climate of the covered galley, the lilac envelopes. I know that awakening in the middle of the night sometimes, watching her sleeping against me, I could feel that the time had come to tell her about it, to make her mine again once and for all through a total acceptance of my slowly woven web of love. I didn't do it because Luciana was sleeping, because Luciana was awake, because that Tuesday we were going to the movies, because we were looking for a car for our vacation, because life came in great screenings before and after the dusk where the grayish light seemed to condense her perfection in the pause in the wicker chair. Because she spoke to me so little now, because sometimes she would look at me again as if searching for some lost thing, I held back the obscure necessity to confide the truth to her, to explain at last the chestnut hair, the light in the gallery. I didn't have time, a chance change in schedules brought me downtown one forenoon and I saw her coming out of a hotel, I didn't recognize her when I recognized her, I didn't understand when I understood that she was coming out holding tightly onto the arm of a man who was taller than I, a man who leaned over a little to kiss her on the ear, to brush his curly hair against Luciana's chestnut hair. (*A Change of Light*, 257–58)

The story dwells on the themes of relativism and the discrepancy between outer and inner worlds. It is a truncated, indirect form of fiction in which the reader has to fill in the gaps to understand the love affair between Tito and Luciana. Not surprisingly, readers without patience to seek out the hidden complexities of elliptical narration tend to dislike "A Change of Light." They fail to find a sense of development or proper closure. But those who allow Cortázar to follow his path soon realize that the story is not devoid of significance; on the contrary, Tito and Luciana's liaison evidences the fracture between fame and private life, between public appearance and private intimacy.

In "The Health of the Sick," a more explicit, overt tale, middle-class family members, knowing their mother is physically ill and unable to cope with bad news, decide to hide the tragic death of Uncle Alejandro. When the mother in turn is about to die, she reveals her own secret knowledge of his death. The story is about guilt and remorse. It is similar to "Letters from Mama," set in Paris and Buenos Aires. Luis, an interior designer, left his hometown years ago in order to awaken his life. He now lives with Laura, also Argentine, a woman once married to Luis's dead brother. Luis's mother, a mature woman living alone in the Flores district of Buenos Aires, asks how they are and tells Luis his brother Nico misses him. The past recurs in Luis's and Laura's lives. From Buenos Aires the mother tells them Nico is about to leave for Europe and will meet them at a train station on a specific date. The couple is terrified but Luis decides to go to the station. In both stories Cortázar is interested in analyzing the tense dynamic within a family: his goal, obvious from the start, is to comment on the many truths, at times conflicting, that reign in any group of people; and his long-standing obsession with alternative (e.g., intuitive, even subversive) ways of knowledge once again finds an expression here. Although we know little about his adult relationships with his sister Ofelia and his mother, Cortázar's ongoing interest with family secrets and intimate lives suggest a writer akin to collective psychology, an artist possessed by the dichotomy between what we known and what we think we know about others.

These three texts—"A Change of Light," "The Health of the Sick," and "Letters From Mama"—bring to mind one of Cortázar's early stories also about gut feelings and about the gap between individual perspective and imagination: "La puerta condenada" (The Blocked Door), still unavailable in English, in which Petrone, the protagonist, a businessman working in Montevideo, stays at the downtown Hotel Cervantes. (Cortázar often used doors in titles and as symbols of alternative realities.) The name of the hotel is not gratuitous: after all, the story is about the limits of reality and the beginnings of schizophrenia (i.e., fiction). He is given a room with a locked door once used to communicate between two dormitories. While the hotel manager has assured Petrone his only neighbor is a single woman, the first night he is awakened by the a crying baby. The disturbances recurs the following night. Petrone complains, but he is again assured only a woman lives next door and that, through the locked door, only her noises could be heard—never a baby. During the next night, when he hears the noise again, Petrone presses his face against the door and makes noises himself, imitating the baby. The woman screams. The next morning the woman checks out but Petrone, when returning to his room, sees that the key to the neighboring room is gone. Once again, the crying baby is heard. Ambiguity and double meaning, Cortázar's favorite devices, conclude the tale as we are left with a couple of possible explanations: either the tale is a ghost story à la Poe, or Petrone's mind is playing tricks on him.[76]

While "La puerta condenada" belongs to the writer's first creative period. Cortázar seems to have rewritten the plot in his second period: "Story with Spiders," part of *We Love Glenda So Much* and thus written some 20 years after the earlier piece, is set in Martinique, an island in the Caribbean. It analyzes the bizarre experience of two female vacationers who, choosing tranquillity in an almost-deserted tourist place, hear voices in a bungalow next door. Thinking at first it's another pair of female vacationers, they ignore the inconvenience of listening at night to mysterious talk, and perhaps what seems an unexpected visit by a gentleman who makes love to them. At the end, however, when their neighbors leave the resort place and the protagonist believe the noises are gone, just as in "La puerta condenada," the two women hear them again next night, and now feel curiosity about the male visitor.[77]

By the early 1980s Cortázar had fashioned a new world of fiction. His stories had invoked a parallel reality to ours, a world where reality has holes through which we can experience mystical, unconventional, dreamlike events. With the passage of time his 100 or so stories will sort themselves out: those that have risen to the top might be removed to a lower critical scale by others that ask for new readings. Together, his short fiction builds a coherent universe where morality is questioned and where the individual is less unique than Western civilization wants us to think. Furthermore, by the early 1980s, in stories that deal with storytelling, in tales about tales, Cortázar had established a fascinating dialogue with himself. Consequently, it isn't causal that in the dusk of his career he wrote "Diary for a Story." Finished in February 1982 and unfortunately still unavailable in English, the story represents Cortázar's consummation as storyteller. Intertwining a plot and the notes leading to it, the text includes referenes to his friend and Borges's collaborator, Adolfo Bioy Casares, to the Cámara Argentina del Libro, and to Poe's poem to Annabel Lee ("It was many, many years ago, / In a kingdom by the sea, / That a maiden there lived whom you may know, / By the name of Annabel Lee").[78] It is not only a wonderful story about a story—a promiscuous piece shedding light on Cortázar's creative process—but it is also a lesson in how to write short fiction and the doubts and struggles a writer undergoes to compose a tale. Readers cannot escape a Borgesian taste to it; after all, it is writing about the act of writing. But it's also Cortázar at his most intimate: a skeleton of a story, a silhouette on the road to corporeality. In that respect it reminds me of Graham Greene's travel book on how he wrote *The Power and the Glory* (1940); Henry James's introductions to his many novels, which detail his labyrinthine creative process; as well as Rilke's *Notebooks of Malte Lauris Brigge.* And it is also a tribute to Poe and his literary tradition of the bizarre and arabesque, and to Argentine letters as a whole. In sum, it is a celebration of Cortázar's own artistic pilgrimage.

End of the Journey

Cortázar accepted President François Mitterrand's offer to become a French citizen in 1981. He did it while insisting he was not relinquishing his Argentine citizenship, but the event was interpreted as a betrayal by many in Latin America. Since his departure to Europe 30 years before, Cortázar had been attacked by Latin American nationalists for abandoning his heritage. In his final collection of prose poems, *Except Dusk* (1984), he included a number of texts written between 1949 and 1950 that concern his eternal identity dilemma: to live in Paris or return to Buenos Aires—exile or home. Feeling, as he did, an endless searcher for the ultimate paradise, he could not go back: he wasn't an Argentine anymore, had given up his native citizenship. But he wasn't a European either. Like many of the characters of his short fiction, he was now a hybrid, a sum of identities. His life has been made of endless farewells, and he now didn't known where he belonged. His writing was manifesting this identity conflict in an explicit way. In his revealing poem "The Dissimulator" he writes,

> That one who leaves his country because he is afraid,
> he knows not of what, fear of cheese with a mouse,
> of sanity among the insane, of froth on the soup.
> So he wants to change himself like a mannequin,
> his hair he used to glue down with lotion and a mirror
> flies free like an oxtail, his shirt unbuttoned, a change
> of ways, of wines and language.[79]

In 1983 Cortázar traveled to Cuba one last time and then to New York to address the United Nations concerning the *desaparecidos* in South America. He felt lonely and alone, especially now that a strange sickness began taking over his body. He lost appetite, became thinner, and was predisposed to colds. After his divorce from Aurora Bernárdez some 15 years earlier, he had been involved with a number of women and men, engaging in bisexual affairs. Among his companions was Ugné Karvelis, a blond, tall Latvian woman who worked for Gallimard and was director of the Spanish section of that publishing house. She had a son with another man whom Cortázar loved dearly. But they separated. He then got involved with Carol Dunlop. Their relationship was brief—she died in 1983 and, as he told Luis Harss, his solitude was so deep, he began to loose trust in his own writing.

A symbol of liberation for many Hispanics, Cortázar, it has been rumored, probably contracted AIDS when the epidemic was still unknown and in the closet, its details elusive to scientists. A number of Cortázar tales deal with homosexuality, including "Blow-Up," "The Ferry, or Another trip to Venice," and "At Your Service," the latter about Madame Francinet, an old servant woman employed as a baby-sitter for dogs in a wealthy home. When asked about homosexuality, Cortázar answered with a lengthy dissertation on the subject, a history from Greek times to the present social ostracism: "The attitude toward [it] has to be very broad and open one because the day in which homosexuals don't feel like corralled beasts, or like persecuted animals or like beings that everyone makes fun of, they'll assume a much more normal way of life and fulfill themselves erotically and sexually without harming anyone and by being happy as much as possible as homosexual males and females" (Garfield 1975, 46). And he finished by applauding the fashion in which, in some capitalistic societies, they are more accepted. Manuel Puig,[80] Reinaldo Arenas, and Severo Sarduy, openly homosexual, died from AIDS—although only Arenas wanted the world to know the truth.

Whether Cortázar did or didn't die of AIDS is still a subject of debate.[81] He officially died of leukemia and heart disease in Paris, on 12 February 1984, and left no children but numerous imitators and countless literary followers, including Argentines Luisa Valenzuela and Ana María Shua. I remember the morning I read the headline in *Excélsior*, Mexico's leading newspaper: "Julio Cortázar, dead at 69." A continental treasure had been lost, and the sense of sadness was overwhelming. The obituary declared the cause of his death to be leukemia and heart disease. He died in Saint-Lazare Hospital and was buried in Montparnasse cemetery. That same year four more of his books were published: *Nicaraguan Sketches; Nothing for Pehujó*, a one-act play; *Except Dusk*, a collection of prose poems; and a collection of political writings. Shortly thereafter *The Exam*, his 1950 novel, finally appeared.

Ironically, Cortázar, energetic, outspoken, incredibly prolific, died a double death: once as a man and again as a writer. Almost immediately after his funeral, international short fiction began to change and his youthful, experimental prose lost urgency and went out of esteem. It is mainly seen today as a product of the anti-establishment revolution that swept Europe, the United States, and the Third World in the late 1960s and the 1970s. Borges, his teacher and sometime nemesis, survived him by two years, but right after 1986, when he passed away in Geneva, his literary legacy achieved the status of a classic. Cortázar's unconventional style, on the other hand, his love of jazz and his passion for experimentalism, make him a contemporary of the Beat Generation and Alain Robbe-Grillet, who in 1956 inaugurated a new trend in French novel writing subscribed to by Michel Butor, Claude Simon, and Nathalie Sarraute. Nowadays Cortázar's most solid audience, as it has been since *Hopscotch* first appeared, is found among young people and in college courses. Like few others, he seems to embody the refreshing spirit of renewal and innovation that prevailed in the Woodstock generation: art as a liberator, art as an innovator, art as an anti-establishment weapon. And yet, as I've tried to show, Cortázar is anything but a transitory name, a forgotten footnote bringing back memories of the Bay of Pigs and Vietnam era, an accidental talent à la Ken Kesey popular in antiwar demonstrations and an idol of the drugs-for-all youth who characterized the 1960s. He is actually an incredibly accomplished storyteller with a distinct worldview, a masterful cornerstone in contemporary Latin American literature. Simply put, the evolution of the postwar novel and short story written in Spanish and the renewal of south-of-the-border letters that came as a result of the Latin American Boom generation would be impossible without him.

Notes to Part 1

1. Jorge Luis Borges, "Julio Cortázar: Cuentos," *Biblioteca personal* (Madrid: Alianza Editorial, 1988), 9–10; my translation.
2. Evelyn Picon Garfield, *Cortázar por Cortázar* (Mexico: Universidad Veracruzana, 1978), 118; hereafter cited in text. See Cortázar's *La vuelta al día en ochenta mundos* (Mexico: Sigo XXI Editores, 1967), 41. The gaucho, a type of Pampa cowboy, was one of Borges's favorite Argentine motifs; his oeuvre is full of gauchos, and with his friend and collaborator Adolfo Bioy Casares he edited the two-volume anthology *Poesía gauchesca* (Mexico: Fondo de Cultura Económica, 1974). Cortázar rarely invoked the gaucho, but whenever he did the image would invariably acquire a Borgesian tone.
3. José Lezama Lima (*Cinco miradas sobre Cortázar* [Buenos Aires:

Part 1

Tiempo Contemporáneo, 1968]) says, "Both Borges and Cortázar have Basque roots. The fact is important to determine their linguistic manners and verbal devises. That is, one has the feeling that another idiom is inhabiting the Basque language's interior" (11; my translation).

4. See Evelyn Picon Garfield's *Cortázar por Cortázar* and *Julio Cortázar* (New York: Frederick Ungar, 1975); hereafter cited in text.

5. "House Taken Over," in *Blow-Up and Other Stories*, trans. Paul Blackburn (New York: Vintage, 1967); 10, hereafter cited in the text.

6. Funes, by the way, is the protagonist of Borges's masterpiece, "Funes the Memorious" ("Labyrinths"). See Julio Cortázar, "News about Funes," in *Around the Day in Eighty Worlds* (San Francisco: North Point Press, 1986), 168–69; hereafter cited in the text. See also Humberto Constantini, *Háblame de Funes* (Mexico: Editorial Nueva Imagen, 1978).

7. See my "Kafka, Cortázar, Gass," *Review of Contemporary Fiction* 11, no. 3 (Fall 1991): 131–36.

8. "Los venenos," in *Final del juego* (Buenos Aires: Sudamericana, 1964), 21; my translation.

9. "On Feeling Not All There," in *Around the Day in Eighty Worlds*, 17.

10. See Emir Rodríguez Monegal, *Borges: A Literary Biography* (New York: E. P. Dutton, 1978).

11. See Terry J. Peavler, *Julio Cortázar* (New York: Twayne Publishers, 1990): 1, hereafter cited in text.

12. Gabriel García Márquez, "El argentino que se hizo querer de todos," *Casa de las Américas* 145–46 (July–August 1984): 23.

13. Luis Harss and Barbara Dohmann, "Julio Cortázar; or, The Slap in the Face," in *Into the Mainstream: Conversations with Latin-American Writers* (New York: Harper & Row, 1967), 206–45.

14. José Donoso, *Historia personal del "boom,"* with an appendix by María Pilar Serrano (Barcelona: Seix Barral, 1983), 137; my translation.

15. Margarita Flores, "Siete respuestas de Julio Cortázar," *Revista de la Universidad de México* 21, no. 7 (March 1967): 10–13.

16. Jaime Concha, "Criticando *Rayuela*," *Hispamérica* 4, no. 1 (1975); Juan Carlos Curutchet, *Julio Cortázar o la crítica de la razón pragmática* (Madrid: Editorial Nacional, 1972); and Joaquín Roy, *Julio Cortázar ante su sociedad* (Barcelona: Península, 1974).

17. See Gerardo Mario Goloboff, *Genio y figura de Roberto Arlt* (Buenos Aires: Editorial Universitaria de Buenos Aires, 1989).

18. See Saúl Sosnowski, "Julio Cortázar, modelos para desarmar," *Espejo de escritores*, ed. Reina Roffé (Hanover, N.H.: Ediciones del Norte, 1985), 39–62.

19. See John King, *Sur: A Study of the Argentine Literary Journal and Its Role in the Development of a Culture, 1931–1970* (Cambridge: Cambridge University Press, 1986).

20. "Muerte de Antonín Artaud," *Sur* 163 (1948): 80–82.

21. "Un cadáver viviente," *Realidad* 5, no. 15 (1949): 349–50. Reprinted in vol. 2 of *Obra crítica* (Barcelona: Anagrama, 1994).

22. "Notas sobre la novela contemporánea," *Realidad* 3, no. 3 (8 May–April 1948): 24–46; it was followed by "Situación de la novela," *Cuadernos Americanos* 9, no. 4 (July–August 1950): 223–43. Reprinted in vol. 2 of *Obra crítica*.

23. "Sobre Leopoldo Marechal: *Adam Buenosayres:* Editorial Sudamericana, Buenos Aires, 1948," *Realidad* 5, no. 14 (1949): 232–38. Reprinted in vol. 2 of *Obra crítica*.

24. See my book *Anti-heroes: México y su novela policial* (Mexico: Joaquín Mortiz, 1993); forthcoming in English translation from Fairleigh Dickinson University Press.

25. Donald A. Yates has also translated the tale. See *Ellery Queen Magazine* 172, no. 5 (August–September 1993): 24–26.

26. Jorge Luis Borges, "Partial Enchantments of the *Quixote*," in *Borges: A Reader*, ed. Emir Rodríguez Monegal and Alistair Reid (New York: E. P. Dutton, 1981), 234–35.

27. See my Introduction to "Latin America: Private Eyes and Times Travelers," a special issue of the *Literary Review* 38, no. 1 (Fall 1994): 5–20.

28. "La urna griega en la poesía de John Keats," *Revista de estudios clásicos* [Universidad de Cuyo, Mendoza] 2 (1946): 45–91. Reprinted in vol. 2 of *Obra crítica*.

29. Lord Houghton, *Vida y cartas de John Keats*, trans. Julio Cortázar (Buenos Aires: Imán, 1995).

30. Kenneth Silverman, *Edgar A. Poe: Mournful and Never-Ending Remembrance* (New York: HarperCollins, 1991), 139.

31. *Borzoi Anthology of Latin American Literature*, vol. 2: *Twentieth Century: From Borges and Paz to Guimaras Rosa and Donoso*, ed. Emir Rodríguez Monegal (New York: Knopf, 1984), 717–19.

32. It was the translator of *Blow-Up and Other Stories*, the poet Paul Blackburn, from whom Cortázar and his last companion, Carol Dunlop, bought the old Volkswagen minibus camper they used for their 800-kilometer drive from Paris to Marseilles, along the Southern Turnpike, which is described in *Los autonautas en la cosmopista* (1983). The volume of stories contains entries from *Bestiario*, *Final del juego*, and *Las armas secretas*. Out of a total of the 31 entries, only 15 have been translated into English.

33. Here, in chronological order, are the most influential: Néstor García Canclini's *Cortázar: Una antropología poética* (1968) and Graciela de Solá's *Julio Cortázar y el hombre nuevo* (1968) look at Cortázar's creative talents and his view of modern man's existential dilemmas (what Cortázar called "the new man," a utopian entity to emerge in a more equal and fair society); Alfred Mac Adam's *El Individuo y el otro: Crítica de los cuentos de Julio Cortázar* (1971) analyzes the

allegorical, existential, and surrealist elements in the author's stories; Saúl Sosnowski's *Julio Cortázar: Una búsqueda mítica* (1973) is concerned with elements expressing, and therefore implicitly symbolizing, deep-lying aspects of human and trans-human existence; Joaquín Roy's *Julio Cortázar ante su sociedad* (1974) is also an examination of the writer's existentialist roots, mainly based on his readings of Jean-Paul Sartre and Albert Camus, as well as his approach to surrealism; Evelyn Picon Garfield's *¿Es Julio Cortázar un surrealista?* (1975) develops the latter argument; América Martínez Cruzado's *The Philosophic and Mystic Aspects of Poe, Baudelaire, and Cortázar* (1976) studies the writer's romantic worldview, as well as the result of the spell he fell under, perhaps through Borges, of oriental mysticism, especially Zen Buddhism and the Vedanta; Antonio Panells's *Metafísica y erotismo* (1979) is a continuation of Graciela de Solá's thesis on the "new man" and a study of sex and eroticism in Cortázar's oeuvre; Laszlo Scholz's *El arte poética de Julio Cortázar* (1977) analyzes the writer as vanguard artist; Ana María Hernández del Castillo's *Keats, Poe, and the Shaping of Cortázar's Mythopoesis* (1981) expands Martínez Cruzado's studies on Cortázar's romantic weltanschauung and the early influences of Poe and Keats on him; Jaime Alazraki's *En busca del unicornio: Los cuentos de Julio Cortázar* (1983) is a detailed examination of what the critic calls "the neo-fantastic" in Cortázar (i.e., a concern with supernatural events that, unlike the works of H. P. Lovecraft, are not necessarily injected with horror); and, finally, Rosario Ferré, the celebrated Puerto Rican woman of letters who also wrote studies on Felisberto Hernández, a Uruguayan storyteller whom Cortázar admired a great deal, is responsible for *Cortázar: El romántico en su observatorio* (1990), which discusses the writer's oeuvre in the light of the romantic movement, again paying special attention to the Poe and Keats influences.

34. Roger Caillois, *Images, images* . . . (Paris: José Corti, 1966); trans. (Spanish) Dolores Sierra and Néstor Sánchez (Buenos Aires: Editorial Sudamericana, 1970).

35. Luis Mario Schneider, "Entrevista a Julio Cortázar," *Revista de la Universidad de México* 17, no. 8 (April 1963): 24–25.

36. *Hopscotch*, trans. Gregory Rabassa (New York: Pantheon, 1966), 396.

37. See Tzvetan Todorov, *Introduction à la littérature fantastique* (Paris: Seuil, 1970).

38. See my essay "Franz Kafka y Felisberto Hernández," in *Prontuario* (Mexico: Joaquín Mortiz, 1991), 125–30. Also see "Ajedrez para idiotas," in *Antología de cuentos de misterio y terror*, selected and introduced by Ilan Stavans (Mexico: Editorial Porrúa, 1994), iv–xviii.

39. *The Book of Fantasy*, ed. Jorge Luis Borges, Adolfo Bioy Casares, and Sylvina Ocampo: Introduction by Ursula Le Guin (New York: Viking, 1988).

40. Since 1940, editing an anthology of tales of horror, mystery, and the supernatural has become an intellectual sport of sorts for lovers of the subgenre. Italo Calvino prepared one on nineteenth-century writers (*Cuentos fantásticos*

del siglo XIX, 2 vols. [Barcelona: Siruela, 1989]), Alberto Manguel another one (*Black Water: The Book of Fantastic Literature* [New York: Clarkson N. Potter, 1983]). See also my collection *Antología de cuentos de misterio y terror*. My choice of Borges story is "The Gospel According to Matthew."

41. "Don't You Blame Anyone," trans. Alberto Manguel, in *Sudden Fiction International*, ed. Robert Shepard and James Thomas (New York: W. W. Norton, 1989), 49–50.

42. See Roger Bartra's intelligent anthropological study *La jaula de la melancolía* (Mexico: Grijalbo, 1989), which discusses Cortázar's "Axolotl" alongside Octavio Paz's *The Labyrinth of Solitude*. Available in English as *The Melancholy Cage* (New Brunswick, N.J.: Rutgers University Press, 1992).

43. See Michelangelo Antonioni, *Blow-Up: A Film* (London: Lorrimer, 1971; rev. ed., 1984).

44. Much richer in style, the Spanish original reads, "Nunca se sabrá cómo hay que contar esto, si en primera persona o en segunda, usando la tercera persona del plural o inventando continuamente formas que no servirán de nada. Si se pudiera decir: yo vieron subir la luna, o: tú la me duele el fondo de los ojos, y sobre todo así: tú la mujer rubia eran las nubes que siguen corriendo delante de mis tus sus nuestros vuestros sus rostros. Qué diablos!" ("Las babas del diablo," in *Las armas secretas*, ed. Susana Jakfalvi [Madrid: Ediciones Cétedra, 1981], 123).

45. Se Flora Schiminovich, "Cortázar y el cuento de uno de sus cuentos," in *Homenaje a Julio Cortázar*, ed. Helmy Giacoman (New York: Las Américas, 1972), 315.

46. Nicolás Bratosevich, *Julio Cortázar: Antología* (Buenos Aires: Librería del Colegio, 1975).

47. In Antonioni's film, which is only inspired by Cortázar's tale, the photos show a corpse, introducing a murder as part of the plot.

48. See Ross Russell, *Bird Lives: The High Life and Hard Times of Charlie "Yardbird" Parker* (New York: Charterhouse, 1973).

49. According to Susana Jakfalvi, the name Johnny Carter derives from two important saxophonists: Benny Carter and Johnny Hodges. See *Las armas secretas*, 158.

50. While jazz also appears in Cortázar's collection *Ultimo round* (1969), it is hardly Cortázar's sole favorite music; he professed a long-lasting passion for Mozart, Beethoven, Bartók, Bach, and Stravinsky (see, for instance, "Clone").

51. Saúl Sosnowski, "Pursuers," in *The Final Island: The Fiction of Julio Cortázar*, ed. Jaime Alazraki and Ivar Ivask (Norman: University of Oklahoma Press, 1978), 161.

52. Mario Vargas Llosa, "La trompeta de Deyá," *Vuelta* 195 (February 1993): 10. Reprinted in Cortázar's *Cuentos completos*, vol. 1 (Barcelona: Alfaguara, 1994): 13–23; hereafter cited in text.

53. Cortázar's favorite contemporary American novel remained John Barth's *Lost in the Funhouse*.

54. Eduardo Galeano, *Memories of Fire*, vol. 3 of *Century of the Wind*, trans. Cedric Belfrage (New York: Pantheon, 1988), 276.

55. "Letter to Roberto Fernández Retamar," in *Lives on the Line: The Testimony of Contemporary Latin American Writers*, ed. with an introduction by Doris Meyer (Berkeley and Los Angeles: University of California Press, 1988), 76.

56. For a discussion of the topic, see my introduction to Babel's *Cuentos de Odesa y Caballería Roja* (Mexico: Editorial Porrúa, 1992), ix–xxviii.

57. Oscar Collazos, Julio Cortázar, and Mario Vargas Llosa, *Literatura en la revolución y revolución en la literatura* (Mexico: Siglo XXI, 1970), 38–77.

58. See Heberto Padilla, *Self-Portrait of the Other* (New York: Farrar, Straus & Giroux, 1990).

59. The scene is reminiscent of Arthur Koestler's classic *Darkness at Noon*.

60. Octavio Paz, "Laude (Julio Cortázar, 1914–1984)," in *Al paso* (Barcelona: Seix Barral, 19), 64–65.

61. Peter Brook, *The Empty Space* (New York: Atheneum, 1983).

62. Jorge Luis Borges, "Averroes' Search," in *Labyrinths: Selected Stories and Other Writings* (New York: New Directions, 1964), 149–55.

63. Juan Carlos Onetti, "Un sueño realizado," in *Tan triste como ella* (Madrid: Lumen, 1982), 41–58.

64. See my essay "Borges, Averroes y la imposibilidad del teatro," *Latin American Theatre Review* 22, no. 1 (Fall 1988): 13–22.

65. See my essay "Onetti, el teatro y la muerte," *Latin American Theatre Review* 24, no. 1 (Fall 1991): 107–14.

66. "A Country Called Alechinsky," in *Around the Day in Eighty Worlds*, 180–83.

67. See "Roberto Arlt: Apuntes de relectura" and "Felisberto Hernández: Carta en mano propia," in *Obra crítica*, vol. 3 (Madrid: Alfaguara, 1994), 247–69.

68. Quoted by Irving Howe in *Politics and the Novel* (New York: Columbia University Press, 1992), 15.

69. "Return to Solentiname," in *Nicaraguan Sketches* (New York: W. W. Norton, 1989), 110–13. The text was written in February 1983, five years after "Apocalypse in Solentiname."

70. See Ernesto Cardenal's *The Gospel of Solentiname*, 4 vols. (Maryknoll, N.Y.: Orbis, 1979), and the notes to Kathleen Weaver's translation of Cortázar's *Nicaraguan Sketches*, 137–42.

71. Carmen Naranjo (b. 1931) is a Costa Rican author of novels, short stories, poetry, essays, and plays.

72. Samuel Rovinski (b. 1936) is a Costa Rican–Jewish novelist and short-story writer who, along with his wife, Sara, was a longtime friend of Cortázar.

73. Sergio Ramírez (b. 1942) is a Sandinista freedom fighter and later Nicaragua's vice president; he is the author of *To Bury Our Fathers* (1985) and *Stories* (1986).

74. A number of Roque Dalton's works are available in English, including *Clandestine Poems*, ed. Barbara Paschke, trans. Eric Weaver (San Francisco: Solidarity Press, 1984), and *Miguel Mármol*, trans. Katherine Ross and Richard Schaaf (Willimantic, Conn.: Curbstone Press, 1987).

75. Omar Prego, *La fascinación de las palabras: Conversaciones con Julio Cortázar* (Barcelona: Muchnik Editores, 1985), 129; my translation.

76. I included "The Blocked Door" in my *Antología de cuentos de misterio y terror*, 7–14; for a brief discussion of its alternative meanings, see the my Introduction (xiv).

77. See my essay "Julio Cortázar, 'La puerta condenada,' y los fantasmas," *Plural* 17, no. 204 (1988): 86–90.

78. *Deshoras* (Mexico: Editorial Nueva Imagen, 1983): 137.

79. My translation. See the Spanish original: *Salvo el crepúsculo* (Mexico: Nueva Imagen, 1984), 339.

80. See Jaime Manrique's moving memoir about AIDS in Latin American life and letters: "Manuel Puig: The Writer as Diva," *Christopher Street* 203 (Summer 1993): 14–27.

81. See my essay "The Latin Phallus," *Transition* 65 (Spring 1995): 48–68. Julio Ortega, of Brown University, among other specialists, maintains that Cortázar's death wasn't AIDS-related; he believes that after Cortázar took an overdose of aspirin doctors discovered that he had leukemia. Further research is required on the subject.

Part 2

THE WRITER

On the Short Story and Its Environs

Léon L. affirmait qu'il n'y avait qu'une chose de plus épouvantable
que l'Épouvante: la journée normale, le quotidien, nous-mêmes sans
le cadre forgé par l'épouvante. "Dieu a créé la mort, Il a créé la vie,
soit," déclaimait L.L. Mais ne dites pas que c'est Lui qui a également
cré la "journée normale," la "vie de tous les jours." Grande est mon
impiété mais devant cette calomnie, devant ce blasphème, elle recule.

Piotr Rawics, Le Sang du ciel

Horacio Quiroga once attempted a "Ten Commandments for the Perfect Story Teller," whose mere title is a wink at the reader. If nine of
his commandments may easily be dispensed with, the tenth seems to
me perfectly lucid: "Tell the story as if it were only of interest to the
small circle of your characters, of which you may be one. There is no
other way to put life into the story."

This concept of the "small circle" is what gives the dictum its deepest meaning, because it defines the closed form of the story, what I have
elsewhere called its sphericity; but to this another, equally significant
observation is added: the idea that the narrator can be one of the
characters, which means that the narrative situation itself must be born
and die within the sphere, working from the interior to the exterior,
not from outside in as if you were modeling the sphere out of clay. To
put it another way, an awareness of the sphere must somehow precede
the act of writing the story, as if the narrator, surrendering himself to
the form he has chosen, were implicitly inside of it, exerting the force
that creates the spherical form in its perfection.

I am speaking of the modern story begun, one might say, with
Edgar Allan Poe, which proceeds inexorably, like a machine destined
to accomplish its mission with the maximum economy of means: the
difference between the story and what the French call the "nouvelle"

and the English call the "long short story" lies precisely in the success-ful story's insistent race against the clock: one need only recall "The Cask of Amontillado," "Bliss," "The Circular Ruins," and "The Killers." This is not to say that longer stories may not be equally perfect, but I think it is evident that the most characteristic stories of the past hundred years have been created through the relentless elimination of all the elements proper to the novella and the novel: exordiums, circumlocutions, situation development, and other tech-niques; a long story by Henry James or D. H. Lawrence may be as pleasing as one of the stories I have mentioned, but it is worth noting that while these authors enjoyed a thematic and linguistic freedom that, in a certain sense, made their work easier, what is always astonishing in stories that race against the clock is the overpowering way they employ a minimum of elements to transform certain situations or narrative territories into a story with ramifications as extensive as those of the most developed novella.

What follows is based in part on personal experience and will perhaps show—from outside the sphere—some of the constants that govern stories of this type. Consider again brother Quiroga's commandment, "Tell the story as if it were only of interest to the small circle of your characters, *of which you may be one.*" To be one of the characters generally means to narrate in the first person, which immediately places us on an interior plane. Many years ago in Buenos Aires, Ana Maria Barrenechea chided me in a friendly way for using the first person excessively, I think with reference to the stories in *Secret Weapons*, although we may have been talking about *End of the Game.* When I mentioned that there were several stories in the third person, she refused to believe me until I got the book and showed her. We theorized that the third person may have been acting as a displaced first person and that memory tended to homogenize the stories in the book.

Then or a little later, I arrived at another explanation from a different angle; I realized that when I write a story I instinctively try to distance myself by means of a demiurge who will live independently, so the reader will have the impression that what he is reading arises somehow out of himself—with the aid of a *deus ex machina*, to be sure—through the mediation though never the manifest presence of the demiurge. I know that I have always been irritated by stories in which the characters have to wait in the wings while the narrator explains details or develop-ments from one situation to another (an explanation in which the demi-urge cannot participate). For me the thing that signals a great story is what we might call its autonomy, the fact that it detaches itself from its author like a soap bubble blown from a clay pipe. Although it seems paradoxical, narration in the first person is the easiest and perhaps the best solution to this problem, since *narration* and *action* are then one and the same. Even when the story is told in the third person, if the telling is a part of the action, then we are in the bubble and not in the pipe. Perhaps that is why, in my third-person stories, I have always tried to maintain a narration *stricto senso*, without those acts of distancing that constitute judgements on what is happening. I think it is vanity to want to put into a story anything but the story itself.

This necessarily raises the question of narrative technique, the special relationship between narrator and narration. For me, this relationship has always been a polarization. While there is the obvious bridge of language that goes from the desire for expression to the expression itself, this bridge also separates me as writer of the story from what I have written, which, at its conclusion, remains forever on the other bank. An admirable line of Pablo Neruda's, "My creatures are born of a long denial," seems to me the best definition of writing as a kind of exorcism, casting off invading creatures by projecting them into universal existence, keeping them on the other side of the bridge, where the narrator is no longer the one who has blown the bubble out of his clay pipe. It may be exaggerating to say that all completely successful short stories, especially fantastic stories, are products of neurosis, nightmares or hallucinations neutralized through objectification and translated to a medium outside the neurotic terrain. This polarization can be found in any memorable short story, as if the author, wanting to rid himself of his creature as soon and as absolutely as possible, exorcises it the only way he can: by writing it.

This process does not occur without the conditions and atmosphere that accompany exorcism. To try to liberate yourself from obsessive creatures through a mere literary technique might give you a story, but without the essential polarization, the cathartic rejection, the literary result will be precisely that, literary; the story will lack the atmosphere that no stylistic analysis can succeed in explaining, the aura that wells up in the story and possesses the reader the way it has possessed the author, on the other side of the bridge. An effective story writer can write stories that are valid as literature, but if he ever knows the experience of freeing himself of a story the way you rid yourself of a creature, he will know the difference between possession and literary craft; and, for his part, a good reader will always distinguish those that come from an ominous undefinable territory from those that are the product of a mere *métier*. Perhaps the most important difference—I have already mentioned this—lies in the story's internal tension. Skill alone cannot teach or produce a great short story, which condenses the obsession of the creature; it is a hallucinatory presence manifest from the first sentences to fascinate the reader, to make him lose contact with the dull reality that surrounds him, submerging him in another that is more intense and compelling. From a story like this, he emerges as from an act of love, expended, separate from the outside world, to which he slowly returns with a look of surprise, of slow recognition, often with relief, sometimes with resignation. The person who writes this story has an even more attenuating experience, because his return to a more tolerable condition depends on his ability to transfer the obsession, and the tension of the story is born from the startling elimination of intermediate ideas, preparatory stages, all deliberate literary rhetoric, to set in play an almost inevitable operation that will not tolerate the loss of time: the creature is there, and only a sudden tug can pull it out by the neck or the head. Anyway, that's how I wrote many of my stories, including some relatively long ones, such as "Secret Weapons": through an entire day relentless anguish made me work without interruption until the story ended, and only then, without even reading it over, did I go down to the street and walk by myself, no longer being Pierre, no longer being Michèle.

So it can be argued that a certain type of story is the product of a trancelike condition, abnormal according to the conventions of normality, what the French call a "second state." That Poe created his best stories in this state (paradoxically reserving for poetry a cold rationality, or claiming to) is proven more by the traumatic, contagious, and, for some, diabolical effect of "The Tell-Tale Heart" or "Berenice," than by any argument. Some will say I exaggerate when I say that only in an extraorbital state can a great short story be born; they will observe that I am talking about stories whose very theme contains "abnormality," like the stories of Poe that I have mentioned, and that I am relying too much on my own experience of being forced to write a story in order to avoid something much worse. How can I convey the atmosphere that precedes and pervades the act of writing? If Poe had written on this subject, these pages would not be necessary, but he shut the circle of his hell and kept it to himself or converted it into "The Black Cat" or "Ligeia." Nor do I know other accounts that could help us comprehend the liberating, chain-reaction process of a memorable short story, so I refer to my own experience as a story writer, and I see a relatively happy and unremarkable man, caught up in the same trivialities and trips to the dentist as any inhabitant of a large city, who reads the newspaper and falls in love and goes to the theater, and who suddenly, instantaneously, in the subway, in a cafe, in a dream, in the office while revising a doubtful translation about Tanzanian illiteracy, stops being him-and-his circumstances and, for no *reason*, without warning, without the warning aura of epileptics, without the contractions that precede severe migraines, without anything that gives him a chance to clench his teeth and take a deep breath, *he is a story*, a shapeless mass without words or faces or beginning or end, but still a story, something that can only be a story, and then, suddenly, Tanzania can go to hell, because he puts a paper in the typewriter and begins to write, even if his bosses and the whole United Nations scream in his ears, even if his wife calls because the soup is getting cold, even if terrible things are happening in the world and one must listen to the radio, even if he has to go to the theater or telephone his friends. I recall a curious quotation from, I think, Roger Fry: a precocious child who was talented at drawing explained his method of composition by saying, "First I think and then I draw a line around my think." In the case of my stories, it is the exact opposite: the verbal line that will draw them is started without any prior "think"; it is like a great coagulation, raw material that is already taking shape in the story, that is perfectly clear even though it might seem that nothing could be more confused; in this it is like the inverted signs of the dream—we have all had dreams of midday clarity that became formless shapes, meaningless masses, when we awoke. Do you dream while you are awake when you write a short story? We already know the limits of dreaming and waking: better ask a Chinese philosopher or a butterfly. But while the analogy is obvious, the realationship is inverted, at least in my case, because I begin with the shapeless mass and write something that only then becomes a coherent and valid story *per se*. My memory, no doubt traumatized by a dizzying experience, retains those moments in detail and allows me to rationalize them here in the context of the possible. There is the mass that is the story (but which story? I know and I don't know, everything is seen by another me, who is not my conscious self, but who is more important at this moment apart from time and reason); there is anguish and anxiety and the miraculous, because both sensations and feelings are contradictory at these times. To write a story in this way is both terrible and marvelous; there is an exultant desperation, a desperate exultation—it's now or never, and the fear that it might be never enrages the moment, sends the typewriter clacking at full throttle, makes me forget the circumstantial, abolishes surroundings. The black mass takes shape as it advances, proceeding, incredibly, with extreme ease, as if the story were already written in invisible ink and only a sweep of the brush were required to bring it forth. To write a story this way involves no effort, absolutely none; everything has already taken place in advance, at a level where "the symphony stirs in the depths," to quote Rimbaud, which is what caused the obsession, the abominable clot that has to be worked out with words. So, since everything is decided in a place that is foreign to my everyday self, not even the ending presents problems, I can write without pausing, making the episodes come and go, because the resolution, like the beginning, is already included in the clot. I remember the morning when "A Yellow Flower" came to me: the amorphous block was the idea of a man who encounters a youth who looks like him and who begins to suspect that we are immortal. I wrote the opening scenes without the slightest hesitation, but I didn't know where things were going, I didn't even think about the resolution of the story. If someone had interrupted me then to say, "At the end the protagonist will poison Luc," I would have been dumbfounded. At the end the protagonist does poison Luc, but this occurred in the same way as everything that preceded it, like a ball of yarn that unravels as we pull on it. The truth is that my stories do not possess the slightest *literary* merit, the slightest effort. If some of them may last, it is because I have been able to receive and transmit what was latent in the depths of my psyche without losing too much, which comes from a certain experience in not falsifying the mysterious, keeping it as true as possible to its source, with its original tremor, its archetypal stammer.

What I have said may have put the reader on the scent: the origins of this type of story and poetry, as we have understood it since Baudelaire, are the same. But if poetry seems to me a sort of second-level magic, an attempt at ontological possession, not a physical possession as in magic properly speaking, the story has no essential intentions, it does not seek or transmit a knowledge or "message." Still the genesis of the story and the poem is the same: they are born of a sudden estrangement, of a *displacement* that alters the "normal" pattern of consciousness; in a time when modes and genres have given way to a noisy critical bankruptcy, there is some point to insisting on this affinity, which many will consider preposterous. My experience tells me that in a sense a short story like the ones I have been describing does not have a *prose structure*. Every time I have undertaken to revise the translation of one of my stories (or tried to translate a story by another, as I did once with Poe), I have been struck by the degree to which the effectiveness and the *meaning* of the story depend on those values that give poetry, like jazz, its specific character: tension, rhythm, internal pulsation, the unexpected within the parameters of the anticipated, that *fatal liberty* that cannot be altered without an irrevocable loss. Stories of this type are affixed like indelible scars on any reader who can appreciate them: they are living creatures, complete organisms, closed circles, and they breathe. *They* breathe, not the narrator, like poems that endure and unlike prose, which transmits the breathing to the reader, communicates it the way you send words through the telephone. And if you ask, "Isn't there communication between the poet (the short story writer) and the reader?," the answer is obvious: the communication operates *from within* the poem, not *by means of* it. It is not the communication of the prose writer from telephone to telephone; the poet and the storyteller direct autonomous creatures, whose conduct is unforeseeable and whose final effects on the reader do not differ essentially from their effects on the author, the first to be surprised by his creation, a reader surprised by himself.

A brief coda on fantastic stores. First observation: the fantastic as nostalgia. All *suspension of belief* operates as a truce from the harsh, implacable siege that determinism wages on man. In this truce, nostalgia introduces a variation on Ortega's observation: there are people who at a certain time cease to be themselves and their circumstances, there is a moment when you want to be both yourself and something unexpected, yourself and the moment when the door, which before and after opens onto the hallway, opens slowly to show us the field where the unicorn sings.

Second observation: the fantastic demands an ordinary passage of time. Its eruption instantly alters the present, but the door to the hallway remains the same in the past and in the future. Even a momentary alteration in the ordinary reveals the fantastic, but the extraordinary must become the rule without displacing the ordinary structures in which it is inserted. To discover Beethoven's profile in a cloud would be disturbing if it did not soon become transformed into a ship or a bird: its fantastic nature would only be confirmed if the profile of Beethoven endured while the other clouds devolved in their eternal random disorder. In bad fantastic literature, supernatural profiles are usually introduced like instant and ephemeral stones within the solid mass of the usual: thus the woman who has earned the thorough hatred of the reader is justly strangled at the last moment by a fantastic hand that comes down the chimney and leaves through the window without the slightest difficulty, even though the author finds it necessary to serve up "explanations" of the sort involving vengeful ancestors or evil spirits. I will add that the worst of this sort of literature elects the opposite procedure, that is, it displaces ordinary time in favor of a sort of "full-time" fantastic, invading almost every aspect of the scene with a vast supernatural cotillion, as in the popular model of the haunted house, where everything assumes unaccustomed manifestations from the moment in the opening sentences when the protagonist rings the bell until the story lurches to a halt beneath a garret skylight. In the two extremes (insufficient installation in ordinary circumstances and almost total rejection of them), the story sins through impermeability; it works with momentarily justified materials among which there is no osmosis, no convincing formulation. The good reader senses that none of these things had to be there, not the strangling hand, nor the gentleman who determines to spend the night in a desolate dwelling on a bet. This type of story, which deadens anthologies of the genre, recalls Edward Lear's recipe for a pie whose glorious name I have forgotten: take a hog, tie it to a stake, and beat it violently, while at the same time preparing a gruel of diverse ingredients, interrupting its cooking only to continue beating the hog. If at the end of three days the glop and the hog have not formed a homogeneous substance, the pie must be considered a failure, the hog released, and the glop consigned to the garbage. Which is precisely what we do with stories in which there is no osmosis, where the fantastic and the ordinary are brought together without forming the pie we want to enjoy trembling.

The Present State of Fiction in Latin America

In light of the limited time we have tonight, I assume as a given that none of you has taken seriously the title of this lecture—"The Present State of Fiction in Latin America"—unless, of course, you suspect that the word "fiction" may refer more to the lecture itself than to its subject matter. I do not know exactly who is to blame for this title, although I confess—with obvious discomfort—that the list of suspects must be reduced to only two: Ivar Ivask and myself. Since it has been almost a year that Ivar and I have been exchanging letters about this conference, it is difficult to know in what precise moment the idea of this theme came up—whether it was proposed by me in a moment of delirium, or whether it resulted from a refined perversity on Ivar's part, a perversity directed somewhat against me but principally against you. The only thing which is certain is that the title of this talk does not correspond to anything realizable within the time alloted; and even if I were the Editor-in-Chief of *Reader's Digest*, my techniques of synthesis would not suffice to summarize here the present situation of fiction in all of Latin America.

Now then, it happens that in the stories and novels that I have written, the presence of what is called the "supernatural" or the "fantastic" is very strong and constitutes perhaps the dominant feature of my work. If the totality of any narrative work can be classified as "fiction," it is clear that fantastic literature is the most fictional of all literatures, given that by its own definition it consists of turning one's back on a reality universally accepted as normal, that is, as not fantastic, in order to explore other corridors of that immense house in which man lives. For reasons of this kind, which are not based too firmly on logic, as many of you will already have perceived, it occurs to me that this talk can have some meaning if we concentrate its scope in two ways: first, on the exclusive dimension of fantastic literature, and secondly,

From *The Final Island: The Fiction of Julio Cortázar*, edited by Jaime Alazraki and Ivar Ivask. Copyright © 1976, 1978 by the University of Oklahoma Press.

on that region of Latin America which, to date, has provided the greatest number of authors of this type of fiction. I refer to the area of the River Plate—not to its liquid part, of course, but to the two shores which delimit it: Uruguay and my own country, Argentina.

In proposing this partitioning of our theme, concentrating it on fantastic literature, which in turn is concentrated in a specific region of Latin America, I feel that I can count on the full understanding of those of you listening to me. I say this because, unlike other national literatures in which the fantastic appears only as a marginal manifestation, English literature in its entirety, with American literature as its most important projection outside of its original center, is in reality the chosen land of fantastic literature. It should be clear that in mentioning a given literature, one implicitly includes its readers as well, and in this case I know that I am addressing people who have been given the dimension of the fantastic since childhood through a literature which is exceptionally rich in it. This fact will allow us to reduce to a minimum the type of theoretical considerations of the genre of the fantastic which would be indispensable for a French audience, for example, since French literature, and thus readers in France, only accept the fantastic begrudgingly and with difficulty.

I will therefore limit myself to merely adjusting summarily the focus of our common point of view before going on to speak of fantastic literature in the River Plate area. For any sensitive reader the fantastic in literature is transparently clear; but it is also clear that when it comes to defining this perception in logical terms, doubts and difficulties arise which the critics of this type of literature have not yet been able to resolve. A definition of the fantastic in literature has been sought for a long time; personally, I have not seen any which satisfies me—and here I include everything from the merely psychological or psychoanalytical definitions to the most recent structuralist attempts. There is, to begin with, a problem of vocabulary: terms such as "marvelous," "fantastic," "strange," "startling," et cetera, change meanings according to their users. This first uncertainty is followed by another—I refer to the sensation of the fantastic itself when it is given to us through a literary text, a sensation which varies considerably throughout the course of history and from one culture to the next. Given this state of affairs, what can I do tonight to explain precisely that notion of the fantastic which I would like to show you in the literature of the River Plate? Not being a critic, my only possibility is to transmit as best I can my own experiences exactly as they have appeared to me since the time I was a child and just as they have been manifested in a series of stories and novels written over the course of thirty years. I will begin, then, by speaking about myself within this perspective, in order then to go on to other writers from the River Plate area. I realize that the Emily Posts of good social behavior would consider that in choosing this personal approach I am displaying a shocking lack of the most elemental modesty, but I see no other way to illuminate a field which is not distinguished by its clarity. To be honest, I prefer to pass for vain rather than for incomprehensible.

Chance (which for me is already a reference to the fantastic) comes to aid me today, because a short time ago I had to write an article on the influence of so-called gothic literature in Uruguay and Argentina, and that caused me to reflect on the relationship between my own childhood and my future as a writer. I think that it can be stated without fear of error, that except in cases where an implacable education cuts him off along the road, every child is, essentially, gothic; that is to say, that due not only to ignorance but above all to innocence, a child is open like a sponge to many aspects of reality that later will be criticized or rejected by reason and its logical apparatus. In the Argentina of my childhood, education was a long way from being implacable, and Julio Cortázar the child did not ever find his imagination shackled. On the contrary, it was encouraged by a mother who was very gothic in her literary tastes and by teachers who, pathetically, confused imagination with knowledge.

Naturally, the sense of the fantastic in a child's mind is always thick and truculent; and it is only much later, as adults, that some people will come to extrapolate from that first capability of being permeated when confronted with the startling or the inexplicable, in order to feel it and to verify it on much more subtle planes. The passage from the simply "marvelous," such as that which appears in the fairy tales that a child accepts in his earliest infancy, to what is called the "uncanny" only comes at the end of a long process of maturation. For me, in the beginning, the fantastic was an incessant producer of fear more than of marvel. My house, to begin with, was a gothic stage set, not because of its architecture, but because of the accumulation of terrors which were born from things and from beliefs, from the badly-lit hallways and from the after-dinner conversations of the grown-ups. They were simple people; their readings and their superstitions permeated an ill-defined reality, and from the time I was very little I learned that werewolves came out when there was a full moon, that the mandrake was a deadly plant, that in cemeteries terrible and horrifying things took place, that dead people's hair and fingernails kept growing interminably, and that in our house there was a basement to which nobody had the nerve to descend—ever. But curiously, that family given over to propagating the worst tales of terror and dread also maintained the cult of virile courage; from the time I was a child it was demanded that I go on nocturnal expeditions intended to temper me, and my bedroom became an attic illuminated by a stub of candle at the end of a staircase, where fear, dressed as a vampire or as a ghost, always awaited me. No one ever knew of this fear, or maybe they only pretended not to know.

Perhaps because of this, as pure exorcism and without clear consciousness of the compensatory reasons which moved me, I began to write poems and stories of which I prefer not to remind myself, pieces where the lugubrious and the necrophilic seemed very much at home. Since nobody watched over my reading, it did not take me long to devour all the fantastic literature within my reach. In general, it was very poor, and there is a certain irony in the fact that only ten or fifteen years later did I come to know the great authors of the gothic genre in their original languages—authors such as Horace Walpole, Sheridan Le Fanu, Mary Shelley and Maturin, not to mention modern masters such as Ambrose Bierce or Gustav Meyrink. As an admirable exception, however, Edgar Allan Poe did enter through the fearful door of my childhood, as did the Victor Hugo of *Hans of Iceland* and *The Laughing Man*, mixed ingenuously with Fu Manchu and other subproducts of the terrorific genre. Thus, with the way prepared by my childhood and by a natural acceptance of the fantastic in all its many forms, that literature, whether bad or good, found in me a reader like those of another time, a reader soon to play the game, to accept the unacceptable, to live in a permanent state of what Coleridge called "the suspension of disbelief."

Here we arrive at something which goes beyond my personal biography and which encompasses the attitude of almost all the writers of fantastic literature in the River Plate area. When I began to write stories that seemed publishable to me, I had already lived thirty-five years and read thousands of books. Because of this, despite my interest in fantastic literature, my critical sense made me find the mysterious and the startling in terrains very different from the traditional ones, although I am sure that without that tradition I would never have found them. The traces of writers such as Poe are undeniable on the deepest levels of many of my stories, and I think that without "Ligeia," without "The Fall of the House of Usher," I would not have found myself with this disposition toward the fantastic which assaults me in the most unexpected moments and which propels me to write as the only way to cross over certain limits, to install myself in the territory of *lo otro*— the Other. But—and in this there is clear unanimity among the River Plate writers of the genre—something indicated to me from the start that the formal road of this otherness was not to be found in the literary tricks on which traditional fantastic literature depends for its celebrated "pathos," that it was not to be found in that verbal scenography consisting of "disorienting" the reader from the start, conditioning him within a morbid climate in order to oblige him to accede docilely to the mystery and the dread. Of course, this critical attitude is not the sole possession of the novelists or short story writers of the River Plate, and in fact it even precedes our generation. It is enough to remember that during the height of English romanticism Thomas Love Peacock already mocked the gothic genre in his delightful *Nightmare Abbey*, a mockery which reached its peak at the end of the last century in the pages of Oscar Wilde's *The Canterville Ghost*.

When writing fantastic stories, then, my feeling in the face of what the Germans call *das Unheimliche*—the unsettling or the startling— came forth and continues to come forth on a plane which I would classify as ordinary. The fantastic had never seemed exceptional to me, even as a child, and now I had come to feel it as a calling, perhaps a warning originating from areas of reality which Homo sapiens prefers to ignore or to relegate to the garret of primitive or animist beliefs, of superstitions and nightmares. I have said a calling, and in my case it always has been one; there are moments in my life (and they are not exceptional moments; they can occur during a subway ride, in a café, in the middle of reading a newspaper) in which for an instant I cease to be he who I habitually am in order to convert myself into a type of passageway. Something opens up in me or outside of me, an inconceivable system of communicating receptacles makes reality as porous as a sponge; for one moment, unfortunately short and precarious, what surrounds me ceases to be what it was, or I cease to be who I am or think I am, and in that terrain where words can only arrive late and imperfectly to try to say what cannot be said, everything is possible and everything can surrender itself. The variety of eruptions of the fantastic is inexhaustible; in one of my novels, *62: A Model Kit*, the first chapters try to reconstruct one of these multiple terrains of passage.

Part 2

A man hears an insignificant sentence in a restaurant, and suddenly the external reality ceases to surround him and to define him in order to give way to a kind of coagulation of elements which reason would reject as heterogeneous or illogical. Within the character what we could call an instantaneous constellation is constructed, a constellation whose isolated elements do not have, in appearance, anything to do with one another. The force of that constellation is so great that the character surrenders himself to it without consciously knowing it, carried along by forces that manifest themselves in that instant without apparent reason or logical explanation. The reader of the book, who indirectly receives the influx of these forces, will see them act in the course of the novel and influence the destiny of the characters, who, for their part, believe that they act freely and do not suspect that that first constellation already contained the integrally constructed model of which they are mere pieces and means.

All this, which is only one example within the infinite manifestations of that which I understand as the fantastic, is not presented in a traditional manner, that is, with premonitory warnings, ad hoc scenarios and appropriate atmospheres as in gothic literature or modern fantastic stories of poor quality. I repeat that the eruption of the Other happens in my case in a markedly trivial and prosaic fashion. It consists above all in the experience that things or facts or beings change for one instant their sign, their label, their situation in the realm of rational reality. Receiving a letter with a red stamp at the same moment that the telephone rings and that one's sense of smell perceives the odor of burnt coffee can convert itself into a triangle which has nothing to do with the letter, the call or the coffee. Rather, it is because of that absurd and apparently casual triangle that something else slips in—the revelation of a deception or of happiness, the real meaning of an act committed ten years earlier or the certainty that in the immediate future a given something is going to take place. I do not want in any way to say that in all cases that coagulation of heterogeneous elements translates itself into precise knowledge, because then we would be leaving the terrain of the fantastic and it would only be a question of scientifically verifying a system of laws or of rigorous principles of which we were simply not aware. In most cases that eruption of the unknown does not go beyond a terribly brief and fleeting sensation that there is a meaning, an open door toward a reality which offers itself to us but which, sadly, we are not capable of apprehending. In my case I am almost always not up to the message, to the sign that those constellations intend to transmit to me; but their force is such that I will never put in doubt the reality of the messages, and the only thing that I can deplore is my own poverty of psychic means, of capacity for entering into the Other. In the presence of the fantastic the same thing happens to me as happens with certain dreams whose intensity is dazzling. We will remember those dreams in the instant of awakening, but a well-known censorship implacably erases them, leaving us scarcely some raveled threads in our hands and the anguish of having touched closely something essential which, simultaneously, our own psyche shuts off to us. And since I have mentioned dreams, it seems appropriate to say that many of my fantastic stories were born in an oneiric territory and that I had the good fortune that in some cases the censorship was not merciless and permitted me to carry the content of the dreams into words. Curiously, those stories have had more effect on my readers than others, although the readers have no way of knowing their oneiric origin. One could say that the fantastic which they contain comes from archetypal regions which in one way or another we all share, and that in the act of reading these stories the reader witnesses or discovers something of himself. I have seen this phenomenon put to the test many times with an old story of mine entitled "The House Taken Over," which I dreamed with all the details which figure in the text and which I wrote upon jumping out of bed, still enveloped in the horrible nausea of its ending. That story, which I can say without false modesty does not seem very extraordinary to me, has nonetheless been reproduced in numerous languages and continues to fascinate its readers. This leads me to suggest that if the fantastic sometimes invades us in full light of day, it is also waiting for us in that oneiric territory in which, perhaps, we have more things in common than when we are awake.

As you can see, for me the idea of the fantastic does not mean only a rupture with the reasonable and the logical or, in literary and above all science fiction terms, the representation of unthinkable events within an everyday context. I have always felt that the fantastic does not appear in a harsh or direct way, that it is not cutting, but rather that it presents itself in a way which we could call interstitial, slipping in between two moments or two acts in order to allow us to catch a glimpse, in the binary mechanism which is typical of human reason, of the latent possiblity of a third frontier, of a third eye, as so significantly appears in some Oriental texts. There are those who live satisfactorily in a binary dimension and who prefer to think that the fantastic is nothing more than a literary fabrication; there are even writers who only invent fantastic themes, without in any way believing in them. As far as I am concerned, what has been given to me to invent in this terrain has always been carried out with a sense of nostalgia—the nostalgia of not being capable of fully opening the doors which on so many occasions I have seen set themselves ajar during a few fleeting seconds. In that sense, literature has fulfilled and fulfills a function for which we should thank it: the function of taking us for a moment out of our habitual little boxes and showing us, although it might only be vicariously, that perhaps things do not end at the point where our mental habits fix them.

We thus arrive at a stage where, even without a precise definition of the fantastic, it is possible to recognize its presence, at least in its literary manifestations, within a much broader and more open range than in the era of gothic novels and of stories whose trademarks were ghosts, werewolves and vampires. Throughout the course of this century many writers in the River Plate area have contributed considerably to the type of fiction in which the fantastic has those subtle and often ambiguous characteristics that I have tried to sketch in their more general lines tonight. But before referring specifically to these writers, it is necessary to pose an enigma which in itself already seems fantastic and which is contained within this question: Why has the River Plate region been and why does it continue to be a chosen land of Latin American fantastic literature? Of course, writers from Mexico, from Colombia, from many other Latin American countries have written notable novels or stories where the fantastic is present; but it is enough to take a look at the general panorama of our continent to see that it is on the two sides of the River Plate where one finds the maximum concentration of this genre.

Many times critics have looked for the answer to this question; they have spoken of the cultural polymorphism of Argentina and Uruguay resulting from the multiple waves of immigrants; they have alluded to our immense geography as a factor of isolation, monotony and tedium, with the consequent refuge in the startling, the exceptional, in the search for an anywhere, out-of-the-world type of literature. As a participant in that literary current, I feel these explanations to be only partial; and in the end, instead of a rational explanation, the only thing that I can see is once more a mechanism of chance, that same chance which once, and in infinitely greater proportions, concentrated a creative explosion in Renaissance Italy and in Elizabethan England, which made possible the Pléiade in seventeenth-century France, and in Spain the generation of the Golden Age or the poets of the Spanish Republic in the 1930s. Suddenly, and without logical and convincing reasons, a culture produces in a few years a series of creators who spiritually fertilize each other, who emulate and challenge and surpass each other until, also suddenly, there enters a period of drying up or of mere prolongation through imitators and inferior successors.

That chance seems to have manifested itself in modest but clearly perceptible proportions in the cultural zone of the River Plate in a period that runs approximately from 1920 to the present. There, without too many premonitory signs, the dimension of the fantastic bursts forth in the principal works of Jorge Luis Borges. It erupts in Borges with a force so compelling that, seen from outside of the River Plate, it appears to concentrate itself almost exclusively in his works. We in Argentina, however, situate Borges's narrative within a context which contains important precursorial and contemporary figures, and although we are not dealing here with a chronology or detailed criticism, I will give some summary indications to show that even before Borges the fantastic was already a familiar and important genre in our midst. Leaving aside the antecedents, above all the historical ones such as the stories of Juana Manuela Gorriti or Eduardo Ladislao Homberg, faithful inheritors of the Anglo-Saxon gothic tradition with all its good and bad points, I will stop for a moment to take a look at a great Argentine poet, Leopoldo Lugones. A man of unbridled cultural voracity, Lugones found time, in the course of producing numerous books of poetry, to write a series of short stories which he collected under the title "The Strange Forces." Among the stories found in this collection, there is one entitled "The Horses of Abdera" which can be counted among the great readings of my adolescence. In this story a herd of horses that today we would call mutants rises up against the men and ends up by taking possession of the city of Abdera, which will only be liberated at the last moment by the arrival of Heracles, the slayer of monsters. The fantastic appears in Lugones with violent profiles and dramatic atmospheres. Nonetheless, it already contains that trait which I have suggested is peculiar to our literature in this area: a force which does not reside only in the narrative quality, but also in a drive which seems to come forth from dark regions of the psyche, from those zones where reality and unreality cease to confront and to deny each other.

Almost parallel to the appearance of Borges in our literature, a Uruguayan with a shadowy biography and a tragic destiny writes in Argentina a series of hallucinatory stories, many of which are truly fantastic. I am speaking of Horacio Quiroga, author of a book which would profoundly influence the men of my generation and whose title reflects both the merits and the weaknesses of its content: "Stories of Love, of Madness, and of Blood." For Quiroga the fantastic appears in a climate of which Edgar Allan Poe would have approved; to demonstrate this, one has only to summarize the plot of one of his best stories, "The Feather Pillow." In this story a girl dies from what appears to be some sort of anemia that no doctor is able to explain or contain. After the burial her husband and servant return to the death room to put the furniture and the bed back in order. The servant is amazed by the extraordinary and abnormal weight of the feather pillow where the head of the sick girl had rested. The girl's husband cuts the pillow open with a knife and then . . . I will leave it to you to deduce the monstrous and entomological ending of the story. But I would like to add something which is as obvious as it is sad for those who give lectures: any synthesis of a literary text automatically destroys it to the extent that, if such a synthesis were possible, literature would cease to be necessary and it would suffice to have lectures.

In Jorge Luis Borges, the leading figure of our fantastic literature, misunderstandings accumulate, usually to his great delight. I will limit myself here to pointing out that what some literary critics admire above all in Borges is a genius of geometrical invention, a maker of literary crystals whose condensation responds to exact mathematical laws of logic. Borges has been the first to insist on that rigorous construction of things which tend to appear, on the surface, as absurd and aleatory. The fantastic, as it appears in Borges's stories, makes one think of a relentless geometrical theorem—a theorem perfectly capable of demonstrating that the sum of the square of the angles of a triangle equals the execution of Madame DuBarry. Stories such as "The Circular Ruins," "The Garden of Forking Paths" and "The Library of Babel" reflect this type of theorem construction, which would seem to hide a secret dread not only of what Lugones called strange forces, but also of the imagination's own powers, powers which in Borges are subjected immediately to a rigorous intellectual conditioning.

Nonetheless, others of us feel that despite this rational rejection of the fantastic in its most irreducible and incoherent manifestations, Borges's intuition and sensitivity attest to its presence in a good portion of his stories, where the intellectual superstructure does not manage to, nor does it probably want to, deny that presence. When Borges entitles a collection of stories *Ficciones* or *Artifices*, he is misleading us at the same time that he winks a conspiratorial eye at us; he is playing with that old ideal of every writer, the ideal of having at least some readers capable of suspecting a second version of each text. I will limit myself, of necessity, to one example which hits close to home. In his story "The Secret Miracle" Borges plays with the idea that in certain circumstances a man can enter into another dimension of time and live a year or a century during what other men live as a second or an hour. There is already a story based on this idea in a medieval Spanish text, *El Conde Lucanor*, and Borges himself uses as an epigraph to his story a fragment from the Koran which reflects the same concept. The theme is also dealt with in the psychology of oneiric life, which shows that certain dreams encompass multiple episodes that would demand considerable time to be carried out consecutively, and that, nonetheless, the complex plot of such dreams can end, for example, with a shot from a gun which abruptly awakens us and makes us realize that someone just knocked at the door. It is clear that the dream has been integrally constructed in order to lead to that supposed shot from a revolver, a fact which obliges one to admit that the dream's fulfillment has been almost instantaneous while the fact of dreaming it seemed to transpire over a long period of time. In other words, one could say that on certain occasions we slip into a different time, and those occasions can be, as is always the case with the fantastic, trivial and even absurd.

But Borges does not want things to be trivial and absurd, at least not in his stories, and "The Secret Miracle" is based once again on the rational and erudite crystallization of something which others grasp only in its unrefined state. The story relates that Jaromir Hladik, a Jewish writer condemned to death by the Nazis, awaits with anguish the day of his execution by firing squad. This man has written philosophical texts in which the notion of time is examined and discussed, and he has begun a play whose ending suggests that the work is circular, that it repeats itself interminably. On the eve of his execution Hladik asks God to grant him one more year of life in order to finish this play, which will justify his existence and assure his immortality. During the night he dreams that the time has been given to him, but the next morning he realizes that it was only a dream, since the soldiers come and take him to the firing squad. In the moment that the rifles take aim at his chest Hladik continues to think about one of the characters in his play; and in that same moment the physical universe becomes immobile, the soldiers do not shoot, and the smoke of Hladik's last cigarette forms a small petrified cloud in the air. Only Hladik can know that the miracle has been fulfilled and that, without moving from his place, thinking it instead of writing it, he has been granted the year he had asked for to complete his play. During the course of this year Hladik creates and re-creates scenes, he changes the characters, he eliminates and adds on. Finally, he needs to find only one word, an epithet. He finds it, and the soldiers shoot. For them only an instant has passed.

This theme, which we also find in Ambrose Bierce's admirable story "An Occurrence at Owl Creek," is not, as Borges's story might pretend, simply a literary artifice. I have already noted the frequent presence of this theme in literature and in dreams, and I have even included it in a passage of my own story, "The Pursuer"; in my case, however, I have no reason to obscure the authenticity of my personal experience and to create of it an ingenious superstructure of fiction. In my story what happens is exactly the same as what has happened to me various times in analogous circumstances. During a subway ride the main character of "The Pursuer" enters into that state which we call distraction and into which the fantastic tends to slide very easily. In a vague semi-dream state the character reflects extensively on the past, he remembers infinite scenes, he mentally hums a song, the memories start to link themselves together endlessly. When the train stops in a station, the jolt abruptly brings the character back to his normal state; he then realizes that if he wanted to enumerate everything he had thought during those minutes, he would need at least a quarter of an hour—and yet everything took place between two stations situated only about two minutes apart. The subway has served as an exterior clock to show him that during those two minutes he was given fifteen minutes to think, just as during a few instants Jaromir Hladik was given a year to finish his play.

I think that at this point you have an idea of our way of living and writing the fantastic in the River Plate area; and so I can now refer to other Uruguayan and Argentine writers without being obliged to present them in too much detail, since within their differences—which fortunately are very great—all of them partake of that same capability of being permeated by the uncanny which I have tried to sketch. In the case of Adolfo Bioy Casares, for example, irony and a sense of humor replace the geometric constructions that we perceived in Jorge Luis Borges. *The Invention of Morel*, Bioy Casares's most famous novel, is closely related to a long-forgotten book by Jules Verne, *The Carpathian*

Castle. In both cases a man in whom scientific genius appears mixed with a lover's great passion fights against that unacceptable scandal which is the death of a loved one. Instead of resigning himself, instead of giving in to the slow curtains of time, Morel creates a prodigious mechanical model, moved by the ocean tides, which allows him to repeat the past, to find himself once again with the image of his beloved and everything which had surrounded her in life. Those who are satisfied with the novel's final explanation, once the mechanism is discovered, will fail to have understood the permanent ambiguity which is established between the living and the dead, between the bodies and the images. Bioy Casares and Borges are not fans of the chiaroscuro, for while they present their fictions in violent contrasts of light and shadow, they do so in order to provide between the black and white a mysterious range of grays which is left for the reader to tune his eyes to and discover.

I am moved to mention here, already nearing the conclusion of this talk, the name of Silvina Ocampo. Discreet, distant Silvina has written memorable stories which have not always found the following accorded to some lesser works in our part of the world. Of her numerous fantastic stories I will cite one, "The Sugar House," in which a woman sees herself slowly taken over by the personality of another woman who long ago occupied the same house. The progression is presented with an admirable economy of means; through scant details and sometimes imperceptible changes Cristina sees herself becoming transformed into Violeta; she finally assumes the personality of Violeta. Rarely has this theme, which I think I know quite well, of the phantasmal possession of a living being by a dead one been presented with such narrative effectiveness; the admirable thing in Silvina Ocampo is the incessant and extraorinarily varied invention of fantastic climates and her simultaneous lack of interest in exploiting them in the most spectacular way. Her stories always seem timidly to offer an apology, when in reality it is the literary critics who should apologize to her for not having been capable of placing her on the level which she deserves. I think, moreover, that this same apology should be extended to other writers of fantastic themes from the River Plate area, principally to Enrique Anderson Imbert, who has lived among you as a professor at Harvard for so many years and whose works have not attained the recognition they deserve.

But what can be said about the last author I would like to mention on this brief voyage? I am speaking of a great Uruguayan writer named

Felisberto Hernández, who lived a life as marginal and phantasmagoric as his stories, almost all of which are autobiographical, although in Felisberto, biography and imagination were always inseparably mixed. Poor, modest, earning a living as a piano player in cafés, giving concerts in pathetic provincial casinos, living in lugubrious hotels which would then be the setting or the point of departure for his stories—written always in the first person—Felisberto limits himself to demonstrating that that miserable existence coexisted with the marvelous and that this quality did not need special ornamentation or equipment in order to manifest itself at any moment. When he wishes, nonetheless, the fantastic bursts forth like an enormous harmony of sounds or colors, and then we have stories like "The Flooded House": a matron takes Felisberto into her lodging, and upon arriving, he discovers that all the furniture and objects float and move about in the salons and bedrooms, beginning with the landlady, sprawled out on her bed as if in a Wagnerian gondola—the entire scene illuminated by light bulbs placed in baking pans, which the gentle currents of water carry from one side of the house to the other without one's ever being able to know where the piano is or where the dining-room table lies.

I am obliged to stop myself in this chronicle, which I would have liked to continue indefinitely; but since we are not on a subway or in front of a firing squad, it is impossible to put into a few minutes everything that we could say about these subjects. At any rate, you have been able to catch a glimpse of how we sense the fantastic in the River Plate, and perhaps this is the moment to point out that that feeling of the fantastic also seems to have projected itself, until very recently, in our national history. In some way (and here I speak especially of Argentina, which I know better than Uruguay) one could say that my country only attained its independence at the beginning of the last century in order to enter, little by little, into a perspective which separated it more and more from universal reality. At the end of our endless civil wars, which coincided with the beginning of the industrial era and the growing consciousness that not only is no man an island, but that countries are not islands either, Argentina often gives the impression of turning her back on herself, surrendering herself to a narcissistic game of mirrors and delusions. Mutatis mutandis, the entire country cultivates a fantastic history, perhaps thus preparing the soil for what I have tried to show tonight and which mere literary criticism does not suffice to explain.

But in contrast to a literature of the startling, which enriches us in the measure in which it accepts and cultivates a rupture with the excessive pragmatism of reality and reason, history does not seem ever to have received a dose of the fantastic without precipitating the worst catastrophes, because nothing fantastic is usable on a practical plane, and what one allows oneself to glimpse as an incitement to go beyond our hermetically sealed compartments becomes pure deception when one pretends to make it serve everyday reality. I think, somewhat metaphorically, of the attempts made by Heliogabalus or Nero to change the reality which surrounded them, of the fatal caprices of so many Oriental sultans and, almost in our own time, of the unrealizable dream of Ludwig II of Bavaria. In some much less typified and spectacular way Argentine history would seem to have consisted for many decades of orienting its mirrors toward impracticable European models, of allowing itself to be invaded by foreign interests which would suck its blood like Dracula preying on his victims, of ignoring the vigorous and still untamed body of the country in order to cultivate only the hypertrophied head of its capital, Buenos Aires, blind with pride, with opera and with money. In this way many Argentines accepted an existence in which what was truly ours, from the color of our skin to our authentic language, was denied by a Europeanizing education which made us uncertain and vulnerable. At present, at the same moment that I am reading these final lines to you, the house of cards has collapsed, just as all the fantastic dreams in the world's history collapsed, and we are witnessing, in conditions which are almost always horrible, the anguished search for our identity, for our necessary and irreplaceable reality. I know that we will obtain it, because the sole fact of having destroyed the false façade of mirrors is already an irreversible triumph; I also know the price we have to pay for that still uncertain ultimate triumph.

In another talk we will speak of these things, which are very far removed from the fantastic. But the fantastic is something that one must never say good-bye to lightly. The man of the future, such as many of us in Latin America dream him, will have to find the bases of a reality which is truly his and, at the same time, maintain the capacity of dreaming and of playing which I have tried to show you tonight, since it is through those doors that the Other, the fantastic dimension, and the unexpected will always slip, as will all that will save us from that obedient robot into which so many technocrats would like to convert us and which we will not accept—ever.

Letter to Roberto Fernández Retamar

Saignon (Vaucluse)
May 10, 1967

My dear Roberto,

I owe you a letter and also some pages I promised you for the magazine on the situation of the intellectual in Latin America today. As you will see almost immediately, it was easier for me to combine both things; if I can just talk to you—even from a piece of paper sent across the sea—I think I can say a few things that would come out too starchy if I put them in the form of an essay, and you know that starch doesn't agree with me very well. Let's just imagine that we're back in the car together headed for Trinidad and that we've managed to grab the best seats for ourselves, to Mario's annoyance, with Ernesto and Fernando jammed in the back, and that we're just continuing that conversation we kept up for three marvelous days last January and which you and I will always find a way to keep going.

I prefer this tone because words like "intellectual" and "Latin American" automatically make me put up my guard, and if they happen to appear together they immediately sound to me like somebody's dissertation bound (I almost said "bound and gagged") in Spanish leather. Add to this the fact that I've been away from Latin America for almost sixteen years and that I consider myself above all a *cronopio* who writes stories and novels with no other objective than the one pursued by all *cronopios*—their own personal enjoyment. I have to make a great effort to understand that despite those peculiarities I am a Latin American intellectual. And I hasten to tell you that until just a few years ago that classification aroused in me the muscular reaction of making me shrug my shoulders until they touched my ears; I think the everyday facts of this reality that oppresses us (*reality* this unreal nightmare, this dance of idiots at the edge of the abyss?) make it necessary to quit playing games, especially word games. I agree then to accept my status as a Latin American intellectual, but I must make one qualification: it is not on account of my being one that I will say what I intend to say here. Circumstances place me in this context and I must speak within it, but I would like to have it understood that I do so as a moral being—let us say as plainly as possible, as a man of good faith, without my nationality and my vocation being the factors determining my words. That my books have been present for years in Latin America does not invalidate the deliberate and irreversible fact that I left Argentina in 1951, and that I continue to reside in a European country for no other motive than my sovereign desire to live and write in the way that seems the most complete and satisfying to me. Certain events of the past five years have moved me to renew my personal contact with Latin America, and that contact has been made because of Cuba and from Cuba. But the importance that that contact has for me does not stem from the fact that I'm a Latin American intellectual; on the contrary, I assure you that it stems from a concern that is more European than Latin American, more ethical than intellectual. If what follows is to be of any worth, I have to be totally frank, so I had to start out by saying these things to the die-hard nationalists who have often reproached me directly or indirectly for my "distance" from my country, for my refusal to physically return to it.

In the last analysis, you and I know very well that the problem facing the intellectuals of our times is the single, universal one of achieving a peace based on social justice, and that preoccupation with the national origins of individuals only subdivides the problem without changing its character. An author far away from his country necessarily has a different perspective on things. When a writer lives at the periphery of local circumstances, outside the inevitable dialectic of daily challenge and response provoked by the political, economic and social problems of a particular country, which demand an immediate commitment on the part of the conscientious intellectual, his sense of the human process becomes more planetary; it operates by synthesis, attempting to see things whole. If this global perspective means loss of concentrated force in an immediate context, it affords a lucidity that is sometimes unbearable but always instructive. It is obvious that as far as mere world information is concerned, it doesn't matter whether you live in Buenos Aires, Washington, or Rome, whether you're living in your own country or outside it. But I'm not talking about information but about vision. As a Cuban revolutionary you know very well that local imperatives, your country's daily problems, form a vital first circle in which you must operate as a writer, and that this first circle, in which your life and your destiny are at stake as well as the life and destiny of your people, is at the same time a point of contact and a barrier with respect to the rest of the world—contact because our battle is that of humanity, and barrier because in a battle it is not easy to attend to anything but the line of fire.

I know there are writers with full awareness of their national mission who also struggle for something that transcends and universalizes that mission; but there are many more intellectuals who, yielding to the conditioning of circumstances, act from the outside inward, latching onto a set of universal ideals and principles and making a country, a language, a national character conform to them. I am not advocating a watered-down, abstract universalism—people becoming "citizens of the world" in order to avoid concrete responsibilities in places like Viet Nam, Cuba, all of Latin America—the sort of universalism that is more comfortable because it is less dangerous. On the contrary, my own personal situation tends to make me participate in what is happening to us *all*, to make me attentive to all voices that approach the compass rose, whatever their angle of origin. At times I wonder what my work would have been like if I had remained in Argentina; I know that I would have continued writing because I'm no good at anything else, but judging by what I had done by the time I left my country, I am inclined to believe that I would have continued along the crowded thoroughfare of intellectual escapism I had traveled until then and which is still the path of a great many Argentine intellectuals of my generation and my tastes. If I had to enumerate the causes for which I am glad I left my country (and let it be very clear that I am only speaking for myself as an individual and not as any sort of model), I believe the main one would be the Cuban revolution. For me to become convinced of this it's enough to just talk from time to time with Argentine friends who pass through Paris evincing the saddest ignorance of what is really happening in Cuba; all I have to do is glance at the newspapers read by twenty million of my compatriots: that's enough to make me feel protected here from the influence that is wielded by U.S. information in my country and which an infinite number of Argentine writers and artists of my generation do not escape, even though

they sincerely think they do; every day they are stirred by the sublimi-
nal mill wheels of United Press and "democratic" magazines that march
to the tune of *Time* or *Life*.

I'd like now to speak in the first person since what has been asked
for is a personal testimony. The first thing I will mention is a paradox
that may be of value if it is considered in the light of the previous
paragraphs, in which I have tried to clarify my situation and your
situation. Doesn't it seem really paradoxical to you that an Argentine
oriented from birth almost entirely toward Europe, to the point of
burning his ships and going to France, without a clear idea of his
destiny, should have discovered here, after a decade, his true condition
as a Latin American? But this paradox raises a deeper question:
Whether or not it was necessary to be situated in the most universal
perspective of the Old World, from which everything seems to be
perceived with a kind of mental ubiquity, in order to gradually discover
a little the real roots of what is Latin American without thereby losing
a global vision of history and man. Age and maturity are factors, of
course, but they are not sufficient to explain that process of reconcilia-
tion and recovery of original values; I insist on believing (and I'm
speaking for myself and only for myself) that if I had remained in
Argentina, my maturity as a writer would have been translated another
way, probably more perfect and satisfactory for literary historians, but
certainly less provocative, challenging, and in the last analysis, fraternal
for those who read my books for vital reasons and not with an eye on
a file card or an aesthetic classification. Here I would like to add that
in no way do I believe myself to be an example of that "return to the
roots," national telluric, or whatever, so characteristic of a main current
of Latin American literature—for example, *Los pasos perdidos* or, more
specifically, *Doña Bárbara*. This atavism as it is understood by someone
like Samuel Feijoó, for example, seems profoundly alien to me because
it is so narrow, parochial, and I would even say provincial; I can understand it and admire it in people who don't achieve, for a multitude of
reasons, a global vision of culture and history, and who concentrate all
their talent on a "regional" focus, but it seems to me to be a preamble
to the worst advances of a negative nationalism when it becomes an
article of faith for writers who because of a cultural deficit insist on
exalting the values of the "land" against values in general, raising up
their country against the rest of the world, their people (because this
is what it comes down to) against other peoples. Can you imagine a

man of the stature of Alejo Carpentier converting the thesis of his above-mentioned novel into a belligerent battle standard? Of course not, but there are those who do just this, just as there are circumstances in the life of a people in which that sentiment of return, that almost Jungian archetype of the prodigal son, of Odysseus at the end of his voyage, can lead to an exaltation of what is theirs in which, through a kind of breakdown of logic, they feel the profoundest scorn for everything and everyone else. And then we know what happens, what happened in 1945, and what can happen again.

Let's say, then, getting back to me, since I am, reluctantly, the theme of these pages, that the paradox of rediscovering from a distance the essence of what is Latin American implies a process that is very different, not at all like a hasty, sentimental return to one's old stamping grounds. Not only have I not returned to my old stamping grounds but France, which is my home, continues to seem to me the ideal place for a temperament like mine, for tastes like mine, and I hope, for what I still intend to write before I devote myself exclusively to old age, a complicated and absorbing activity, as we know. When I say that I was privileged to discover my condition as a Latin American, this was only one of the aspects of a more open and complex evolution. This is not an autobiography, so I'll summarize that evolution by simply enumerating its stages. A writer left Argentina who believed, as Mallarmé did, that reality ought to culminate in a book; in Paris a writer was born who believed that books ought to culminate in reality. That process embraced many battles, defeats, betrayals and partial successes. I began by becoming more aware of my fellow man on a sentimental and, in a manner of speaking, anthropological plane; one day I woke up in France to the abominable evidence of a war in Algiers—I who as a boy had understood Spain's war and later the World War as events in which what was essentially at stake were ideas and principles. In 1957 I began to be aware of what was happening in Cuba (previously through news articles from time to time, I had gained a vague notion of a bloody dictatorship like so many others, but I had no strong commitment of feeling, despite my sympathy for the principles involved). The triumph of the Cuban revolution, the first years of the government, were no longer a mere historical or political satisfaction; suddenly I felt something else, an incarnation of the cause of man as I had finally come to understand it and yearn for it. I understood that socialism, which until then had seemed to be an acceptable and even necessary historical current, was the only current in modern times that was based on the essential facts of human existence, on the fundamental ethos that was systematically ignored in the societies in which it had been my destiny to live—the simple yet inconceivably difficult principle that humanity will begin to be worthy of its name on the day in which the exploitation of man by man comes to an end. I was incapable of going further than that, because, as I have told you and demonstrated to you on many occasions, I am completely ignorant of political philosophy; I have not come to feel myself a writer of the left as a result of an intellectual process but as a result of the same mechanism that makes me write the way I write or live the way I live—a state in which intuition, some magical sharing of the rhythm of men and things, charts my course without giving or asking explanations. With Manichaean oversimplification I can say that almost every day I run into people who are thoroughly familiar with Marxist philosophy and who nevertheless behave on a personal plane in a completely reactionary manner, while I, who have been steeped in bourgeois philosophy my whole life long, nevertheless venture farther and farther along the avenues of socialism. And what is being asked about in this present survey is by no means easy to define—the *situation* in which I find myself at the moment. A text of mine, "Casilla del camaleón," recently published in your magazine, could demonstrate a part of that permanent conflict of the poet with the world, of a writer with his work.

But returning to my situation as a writer who has decided to assume a task he considers indispensable in the world around him, I want to complete the description of the road that ended in my new awareness of the Cuban revolution. When I was invited to visit your country for the first time, I had just read *Cuba, Prophetic Island* by Waldo Frank, which struck a responsive chord in me, awakening a kind of nostalgia. I felt a sense of lack, as if I were out of touch with the world of my times, although in those years my Parisian world was as full and exultant as I had always wanted it to be, something I had achieved after more than a decade of living in France. Personal contact with the achievements of the revolution, friendship and dialogue with writers and artists, everything I saw, positive and negative, on that first trip had a double impact on me: on one hand I was again touching Latin America, from which I felt so far away at the personal level, and on the other hand I was witnessing the hard and at times desperate task of building socialism in a country so ill prepared for it in many ways, so open to the most imminent danger. But then I realized that that double experience actually wasn't double at all, and that sudden discovery amazed me.

Without previous analysis, without thinking about it, I suddenly came to the marvelous realization that my ideological path coincided with my return to Latin America; the revolution, the first socialist revolution I was privileged to follow firsthand, happened to be a Latin American revolution. I hope that on my second visit I showed you that my amazement and joy did not remain on the level of mere personal satisfaction. I felt that somehow my belief in a socialist future for humanity and my individual and emotional return to Latin America, which I had left without a backward look many years earlier, were finally reconciled.

When I returned to France after those two trips, I understood two things much more clearly. On one hand, my personal and intellectual commitment to the fight for socialism, which up to that time had been rather vague, would enter, as indeed it did enter, a phase of concrete definition, of personal collaboration wherever I could be of use. On the other hand, my work as a writer would continue on the course that my character and temperament set for it, and although at some moment it might reflect that commitment (like an occasional story that takes place in your part of the world), this would be a consequence of the same principles of aesthetic freedom that are leading me at the present moment to write a novel that is set almost outside of historical time and space. At the risk of disappointing the catechists and the defenders of art at the service of the masses, I continue to be that *cronopio* who, as I said at the beginning, writes for his own pleasure or his own personal suffering, without the slightest concession, without "Latin American" or "socialist" obligations understood as a pragmatic a priori. And it is here that what I tried to explain at the beginning finds its greatest justification. I know very well that living in Europe and writing as an "Argentine" scandalizes those who demand a kind of obligatory classroom attendance for the writer. Once to my utter stupefaction a foolish jury awarded me a prize in Buenos Aires; I found out that a certain celebrated woman novelist from those parts had said with patriotic indignation that Argentine prizes ought to be given only to residents of the country. This anecdote epitomizes in all its stupidity an attitude that appears in many forms but which always has the same objective: even in Cuba, when it could make little difference whether I live in France or in Iceland, there are those who are mildly disturbed about my supposed exile. False modesty is not my forte. It astonishes me at times that people don't see that the reason my books have had some resonance in Latin America is that they postulate a literature whose national and regional roots are nourished by a more open and complex experience of reality; each evocation or re-creation of what was originally my experience reaches its maximum tension precisely when it opens outward onto and inward from a world that transcends it—a world which, in the last analysis, chooses it and perfects it. What Lezama Lima has done in Cuba, that is, assimilate and Cubanize in a poetic synthesis the heterogeneous elements of a culture that embraces everything from Parmenides to Serge Diaghilev, I would like to do through tangible experiences, direct contacts with a reality that has nothing to do with information or erudition, but which is its *living* equivalent, the lifeblood of Europe. And if one could say about Lezama Lima, as Vargas Llosa has just done in a beautiful essay appearing in the magazine *Amaru*, that his Cubanness is profoundly affirmed by his assimilation of foreign elements into the vital juices, the very voice of his country, I also feel that the Argentinity of my work has gained rather than lost because of this spiritual osmosis. A writer in this state neither renounces nor betrays anything. Rather, he establishes a vantage point from which his original values become part of a perspective infinitely wider and richer. From it, these values—as I know very well, although others may deny it—gain in richness, in amplitude, recovering the deepest and most valuable elements they have to offer.

Because of all this you will understand that my "situation" doesn't concern me simply on the personal plane; I am quite willing to go on being a Latin American living in France. Exempt for the moment from any kind of coercion, from the censorship or self-censorship that restricts the expression of those who live in highly polarized environments, my problem continues to be, as you must have sensed when you read *Rayuela*, a metaphysical problem, a continual struggle between the monstrous error of being what we are as individuals and as people of this century, and the possibility of an ideal: a future in which society will finally culminate in that archetype of which socialism provides a practical vision and poetry provides a spiritual one. From the moment I gained awareness of the essential human condition, the quest for that ideal has been my commitment and my duty. But I no longer believe, as I once could, so comfortably, that literature of mere imaginative creation is sufficient to make me feel that I have fulfilled myself as a writer; my notion of that literature has changed. I now believe that that literature embraces the possibility of representing the conflict between individual realization as humanism understood it, and collective realization as socialism understands it—a conflict that achieves what is perhaps its most devastating expression in Peter Weiss's *Marat-Sade*. I will never write expressly for any one faction, minority or majority, and the repercussion that my books may have will always be a secondary phenomenon unrelated to my task. Nevertheless, I now know that I write *for the sake of, in order to*, that there is an intentionality directed toward a hoped-for reader in whom the seed of the future man resides. I cannot be indifferent to the fact that my books have encountered a vital response in the young people of Latin America. This strikes me as the confirmation of a potential, the possibility of insights, intimations—apertures upon mystery, wonder, the astonishing beauty of life. I know of writers who surpass me in many ways and whose books, nevertheless, do not engage the people of our lands in the fraternal combat that mine do. The reason is simple. If, once upon a time, a man could be a great writer without feeling like a participant in the immediate history of mankind, this is no longer true. No one can write today without this participation: it is a responsibility and an obligation. Works that assume this obligation, even though they are imaginative works displaying the entire gamut of games writers can invent, are the only ones that can approach greatness. Even though they never allude directly to that participation, in some ineffable way they will contain that tremor, that presence, that atmosphere that makes them recognizable and enduring and awakens in the reader a sense of contact and closeness.

If this is still not sufficiently clear, let me add an example. Twenty years ago I saw in Paul Valéry the highest exponent of Western literature. Today I still admire him as a poet and essayist, but he no longer represents that ideal for me. No one could represent it who, throughout a lifetime dedicated to meditation and creation, arrogantly ignored the dramas of the human condition which were given expression in the eponymous work of an André Malraux, and which in a devastating, contradictory way, but in a way that was far more admirable precisely because of the devastation and the contradictions, were being portrayed by an André Gide. I insist that I demand of no writer that he make himself a tribune of the struggle being waged against imperialism in its many forms; but I do demand that he be a *witness* of his own times as Martínez Estrada and Camus tried to be, that in his work or in his life (how can they be separated?) he bear witness in his own way. It's no longer possible to respect, as we once could, the writer who takes refuge in an ill-conceived freedom in order to turn his back on his own human sign, his pitiable and marvelous condition as a man among men, of a privileged spirit among the martyred and the dispossessed.

For me, Roberto, and with this I will close, none of this is easy. The slow, absorbing, infinite and egoistic traffic with beauty and culture—life on a continent where a few hours put me in front of a fresco by Giotto or a Velázquez at the Prado, the curve of the Rialto of the Grand Canal or those London salons in which it seems that the paintings of Turner reinvent light, the daily temptation to return as in other days to a total, feverish absorption in intellectual and aesthetic problems, to lofty games of thought and imagination, to creation with no other finality than the pleasure of the intellect or the senses—all this sets off in me an interminable battle with the feeling that none of it is ethically justified if at the same time it is not open to the vital problems of peoples, if it does not resolutely assume the condition of the intellectual of the third world to the extent that every intellectual nowadays potentially or effectively *belongs to the third world, since his mere vocation is a danger, a threat, a scandal for those who are slowly but surely resting a finger on the trigger of the bomb.* Yesterday in *Le Monde*, a cable from UPI transcribed the declarations of Robert McNamara. These are the exact words of the U.S. Secretary of Defense: "We consider that the explosion of a relatively small number of nuclear devices in fifty urban centers of China would destroy half the urban population (more than fifty million persons) and more than half of the industrial population. Moreover, the attack would eliminate a large number of persons occupying key positions in government, in technical areas and in industrial management, along with a high proportion of skilled workers." I quote this paragraph because I think that after reading it, no writer worthy of the name would be able to return to his books as if nothing had happened. I cannot keep writing with the comfortable feeling that a writer's mission is accomplished in the mere exercise of a vocation as novelist, poet or dramatist. When I read such a paragraph, I know which of the two elements of my nature has won the battle. Incapable of political action, I do not renounce my solitary cultural vocation, my obstinate ontological search, the games of the imagination in their most dizzying planes. But all this does not merely revolve about itself; it no longer even resembles the comfortable humanism of the Mandarins of the West. In the most gratuitous thing I might write there will always appear a will to make contact with the historical present of man, to share in his long march toward excellence as a collectivity and as humanity. I

105

Part 2

am convinced that only the work of those intellectuals who respond to that impulse and that rebellion will become part of the consciousness of peoples and so justify this profession of writing for which we were born.

A very strong *abrazo* from your

JULIO

106

Part 3

THE CRITICS

Introduction

The two essays in this section expose the reader to different approaches to Julio Cortázar's first and second creative periods (1945–66 and 1967–83) as a short-story writer, and they often reach conclusions quite different from my own. John Ditski examines the writer's early fiction, particularly *End of the Game*. Developing a theme that runs through my Part 1, he perceives Cortázar as a Borges disciple and discusses the influences on the author of "Tlön, Uqbar, orbis tertius" on Cortázar. He does a detailed reading of almost every story in the volume, concluding that it is in the fantastic (*lo fantástico*) where the two depart: in Cortázar "the fantastic breaks through masks of the 'real' through holes in time . . . whereas in Borges, they do through magic holes in space." Evelyn Picon Garfield's essay serves as a companion to Ditski's: it explores Cortázar's later short fiction, particularly the pieces included in *Octaedro*, most of which appeared in English in *A Change of Light and Other Stories*. (Unlike me, she approaches *Cronopios and Famas* as fiction.) Her analysis is insightful and explores many stories I only referred to in passing in Part 1. She concludes with a discussion of Cortázar's novelistic reach and suggests that characters in his work function as unidentified narrators and guides to the readers, and that they provide them with the basic clues for interpretation.

John Ditski

In Emir Rodríguez Monegal's 1978 biography *Jorge Luis Borges* (New York: Dutton), attention is drawn to a lecture Borges gave in Montevideo in 1949—a lecture in which the Argentinian master "outlined four procedures which allow the writer to destroy not only the conventions of realistic fiction but also those of reality." Those procedures are "the dream, travel through time, and the double" and, heading the list, "the work of art inside the work of art" (406). The same list is cited in James E. Irby's Introduction to the important selections of Borges in English, *Labyrinths* (New York: New Directions, 1964, xviii); but in his Preface to the same edition, André Maurois presents his own compilation of basic Borgesian ideas:

> . . . that of Endless Recurrence, or the circular repetition of all the history of the world . . . ; that of the dream within a dream; that of centuries that seem minutes and seconds that seem years . . . ; that of the hallucinatory nature of the world. (xii)

It will be seen at once that these lists are both overlapping and even arguably internally redundant. The important thing, however, is their essential correctness as far as Borges' own work is concerned, as well as their applicability to that of his younger disciple Julio Cortázar. This paper will concern itself with the volume of short stories—we might as well employ the Borgesian term "fictions" to describe them—which were published in the United States in 1963 under the collective title *End of the Game*. Compiled from as many as three different Spanish-language collections of Cortázar's writing, *End of the Game* is nevertheless an appropriate place to look for Borgesian influences upon Cortázar. But this is not a study in influences; rather, it is an inquiry into the way a Cortázar story typically works—even stories as apparently diverse as those collected in *End of the Game*.

From John Ditski, "*End of the Game*: The Early Fictions of Julio Cortázar," *Review of Contemporary Fiction* 3, no. 3 (Fall 1983); 38–44. © 1983 by the Review of Contemporary Fiction.

After stating his recapitulation of Borges' favorite devices, Rodríguez Monegal observes that one might be tempted to see them as ˮsubjects" instead of as the "technical devices" they are. But, he concludes, to Borges these approaches "are not just subjects but procedures used in the structuring of a plot. They belong to the formal and not to the thematic fabric of the story" (406–7). If Rodríguez Monegal has made a helpful distinction here—since it is not our intention to discuss the fictions of Cortázar in thematic terms—he has also reminded us of one of the most seductive of literary and critical clichés: the notion of the identity or at least congruity of form and content. Without forcing the issue, I shall want to maintain that for Julio Cortázar as much as for his mentor Borges, if not even more so, fictional plot results from odysseys into the elusively relativistic nature of reality. As with Borges, then, the Cortázar fiction is also by way of being an essay. Quests for understanding initiate processes which the reader is invited to complete. Frequently, the melodramatic norms of detective fiction are quite overturned in Cortázar: the plot advances with the receding of the grail that is "the truth." Frustration attends the reluctant reader who declines the gambit of full participation in the ongoing process which is a Cortázar fiction; for those who join the quest, the uneasy pleasures of a profound disorientation may be the ultimate guerdon.

End of the Game is divided into three sections which have no apparent relationship with the Spanish-language original; nor do the three possess any clear internal coherence beyond the evident fact that the last of the three is the lengthiest and consists for the most part of longer and more conventionally "realistic" stories. There would seem to be no great reason not to proceed with our survey in the order in which the stories appear in the U.S. edition. Since by the word "original" above I mean, in effect, "originals"—a mixing of dates of composition and publication being thus implied—we might as well take these three groups of stories in order, as if they were indeed separate volumes. "Axolotl" is the first Cortázar fiction thus encountered, and it makes for an effective immersion in the Cortázar technique.

Indeed, "immersion" is the appropriate term, for the reader is flung into the fantastic experience of the narrator in "Axolotl," rather in the way babies can be taught to swim by being flung into swimming pools. "Axolotl" concerns a narrator who is obsessed with the salamander larvae known as axolotls, his fascination with them having developed over numerous visits to an aquarium. As early as the story's second page, in fact, he betrays the extent of his empathy with them by confiding that "only I can know how narrow and wretched" is the axolotls' tank. "I knew that we were linked," he states, because "something infinitely lost and distant kept pulling us together" (New York: Harper Colophon Books, 1978, p. 4). The mysteriousness of the axolotls keeps drawing the narrator further "in," to the point of meditating on the axolotls' resemblances to humans—or their lack. In a sudden reversal, the narrator begins to speak of the little creatures as "we" (5). The axolotls with their "Aztec" faces, with their eyes that speak of "a different life, of another way of seeing," seem to be "witnesses," "judges"; the lack of real similarity between their species and human beings somehow underscores what a "profound relation" is being established between the narrator and themselves (6–7). Indeed, the axolotls are said to be devouring him "slowly with their eyes, in a cannibalism of gold" (7). As a result of his obsession with proving to his "own sensibility" that it was "projecting a nonexistent consciousness upon the axolotls" (8), the narrator undergoes a radical transformation: he *becomes* an axolotl. Now "what was his obsession is now an axolotl, alien to his human life," muses the axolotl narrator, looking at the vacated human entity outside the glass of the tank (9). Perhaps, he concludes, that human may even someday write "a story about us, that, believing he's making up a story, he's going to write all this about axolotls" (9). The language is precise: the human creator's delusion that he is in charge of the creative process is ultimately equivalent to his transformation into his subject. The obsessive projection of the creative consciousness involves an entrance into a convoluted state—Borges would have called it a labyrinth—the loopings of which are infinite.

Thus "subject" and "procedure" are one and the same in a Cortázar story. Another permutation of this notion can be found in the next piece, "House Taken Over." For unless it—and by the same token, "Axolotl"—be considered a simple "trick" story (ordinary science fiction, or a tale of "haunting"), the reader must deal with the suggestions of the philosophical that Cortázar has placed within his structure and his texture. Cortázar's titles are apt to lead directly to his stories' cores; and in "House Taken Over" the narrator's primary concern is voiced in the story's very first line. The house is, or was, occupied by a reclusive brother and sister, but it is also identified with the lives that have been lived there before—a succession of memories and events which are to be terminated, in effect by this "quiet, simple marriage of sister and brother" (11). Yet, the brother reminds us, "it's the house

I want to talk about . . ." (11). Two pages later, the narrative reaches
its quick initial climax with the revelation that "it happened": an
unidentified "they" have taken over part of the house, and the brother
and sister are forced to make such a sudden evacuation of those rooms
that certain key possessions—memories? functions?—are left behind
forever. Their lives turn into a spiritless routine of knitting and philat-
ely. Finally, "they" somehow make a second invasion of the siblings'
territory—from "if not the kitchen, then the bath" (16). Frightened,
with nothing whatsoever on their persons and at 11 P.M., the brother
and sister find themselves on the street; our further questions unan-
swered, the story ends abruptly "with the house taken over" (16). The
triumph of the narrator's paranoia, or his reverse-obsession with a life
he cannot cope with, is complete. The sister even abandons the knitting yarn when she observes that she has dropped the balls of yarn on
the other side of a door now closed—in effect surrending the key to
the labyrinth and acknowledging the supremacy of the Minotaur. Aside
from clues dropped early in the story, Cortázar wastes no time on
rationalizations; the abrupt ending accomplishes a resolution through
its lack. Structure equals experience.

In "The Distances," Cortázar takes greater space to deal with a
greater psychological complexity. Alina Reyes tells her own story
through her diary, itself an indication of the interior "distances" that
have begun to open up between Alina and the world around her, or
between one and another aspect of her personality. Though the story
becomes third-person narrative two pages before the end when Alina
closes her diary because she is married—"for one gets married or one
keeps a diary" (25)—she has long since given indications of a sundered
consciousness. For instance, when playing a piano accompaniment for
her sister, she argues against criticism of her playing by noting that "I
watched my hands on the keys and it seemed to me they were playing
all right" (20). Unable to feel herself fully in the world around her,
she allows music to separate her more and more from that world; she
projects a surrogate self who is a beggar woman on the snowy streets
of Budapest, one who knows she is alive because she suffers and is
beaten: "I can only hate her so much, detest the hands that throw her
to the ground and her as well, her even more because they beat her,
because I am I and they beat her" (18–19). The character of these
entries, rather like the interior monologues of Addie Bundren in *As I
Lay Dying*, is the measure of Alina's passivity; she has been shipping
her consciousness abroad, and with it her reality. When the diary ends,

the new narrator tells us that Alina went abroad, to Budapest, with her husband—"two months before their divorce" (26). There she encounters her other self on a bridge; for someone so lacking in a sense of an authentic self, the union is ecstatic:

> Alina ached: it was the clasp of the pocketbook, the strength of the embrace had run it in between her breasts with a sweet, bearable laceration. She surrounded the slender woman feeling her complete and absolute within her arms, with a springing up of happiness equal to a hymn, to loosing a cloud of pigeons, to the river singing. She shut her eyes in the total fusion. . . . (27)

This mystical and musical fusion with the other self, the created double, leads to an "Axolotl"-like exchange of personae: for a moment identities are blurred; and then closed eyes are opened, and there is a scream! But now the narration's "she" is a different person, one watching Alina Reyes, "lovely" now, walking into the wind, "not turning her face. Going off" (27). Again in Cortázar, the creative consciousness has triumphed terribly over the "real."

Cortázar tells "The Idol of the Cyclades" with a melodramatic tinge that might be accounted for by its resemblance to Borges' knife-fight narratives. The twist here is provided by the identification of the power of the past over the present with a cult object dug out of the ground by a team of archaeologists—two men and the wife of one of them. The ending of the story is foreshadowed, when one learns to recognize such events in Cortázar, by the scene of the discovery at the beginning: in her excitement at being called over to the excavation pit, the wife appears without her bikini top; thus the rediscovered idol begins at once to occupy a position at the center of a conventional sexual triangle (29). The unmarried partner, Somoza, becomes obsessed with the idol; as the husband, Morand, explains it, "every archaeologist identifies himself with the past he explores and brings to light. From that point to believing that intimacy with one of those vestiges could alienate, alter time and space, open a fissure whereby one could comply with . . ." (32, ellipsis Cortázar's). Where this unfinished passage leads, of course, is to the story's climax; we find Somoza trying to reenter the mind of the past by recreating its cult objects, in this case making replicas of the idol that finally become so good that they cannot be distinguished from the original (33). Morand watches as Somoza begins to stroke the idol, and hears Somoza begin to speak "in a stifled and opaque voice"

of the concerns of the primitive era which had created the idol (35).
Morand begins to talk wildly about sacrificing a woman to the gods,
hearing, as he says this, the sound of ancient flutes; he then strips off
his clothes and attacks Morand with a hatchet (36–37). Morand is lucky
enough to win the struggle, and Somoza dies a bloody death. But the
story's final twist is provided when, thanks to the bloody "sacrifice"
and the idol being present, Morand himself—his mind simultaneously
operating in two time frames—surrenders to the force of the past; we
see him waiting naked in the darkness, hearing "the sound of the
flutes" and "licking the cutting edge of the hatchet" as he waits for
his wife behind the door. The cult is reborn! And again a story ends
on a note of ostensible imminence that is, in truth, a completion of a
demonstration.

In comparison, "Letter to a Young Lady in Paris" seems at first to
be a kind of comic relief, thanks to the letter's narrator's propensity
for vomiting up bunnies in the apartment of his everything-in-its-
place girlfriend now living in Paris. So matter-of-factly are the bunny-
spittings introduced into the story line that the reader is amused by
the cuteness of the device (41). But the bunnies are equated with
the speaker's habits, themselves "concrete forms of rhythm, . . . that
portion of rhythm which helps to keep us alive" (42). Though "a month
is a rabbit," and though one can kill the rabbits with alcohol (43), the
bunnies are causing damage in the apartment; and the narrator cannot
stop bringing them into existence. Thus the story abruptly turns into
a suicide note, as the narrator—on the verge of vomiting his twelfth
rabbit—reveals his plans to throw the first eleven and, it would seem,
himself from his girlfriend's balcony. Once again in Cortázar the projection of the obsessional self leads to fatal results.

Indeed, in the final story in the first section, "A Yellow Flower,"
the fatality takes the form of the apparent murder of—or complicity in
the death of—a young man encountered by the narrator's interlocutor,
someone who claims to have discovered that "We are immortal" (51).
The source of this discovery is the chance encounter of the speaker's
consecutive replacement—a young man, Luc, who is the speaker reborn, thus doomed to the same failed existence. By having Luc die,
the speaker breaks the eternal chain, and thus becomes the only person
in the world *not* to be immortal. His reaction to his new state, a twist
on a familiar Borgesian notion, is exhilaration. But then he sees the
yellow flower of the title, and realizes that the flower can replace itself,
and is therefore in a sense immortal, but that now he himself must

115

die, " '. . . there would never be anything, there'd be absolutely nothing, and that's what nothing was, that there would never again be a flower' " (59). The story ends with the speaker's recitation of his futile quest for another futile replacement for himself, for Luc—and with the narrator's fatigue. To this narrative, the tragic aspect of which has a distinctive double-bind to it, Cortázar has his reader share his own ennui; the narrative extinguishes itself.

The lead story in the second section, "Continuity of Parks," is only three pages long; but that is space enough for Cortázar to accomplish what will make the story a classic to be alluded to by name for its uniqueness. A reader immerses himself with pleasure in a novel, the plot of which includes a melodramatic meeting of a man and woman in a park. Apparently the man, who is armed with a dagger, will leave the meeting in order to accomplish a murder. Because the reader has surrendered himself to the novel's "glamour" with "almost perverse pleasure," he has been guilty of complicity in the book's events, and we are perhaps not surprised to find that the man whom the armed man intends to kill is the man in the chair reading towards his own doom. Seldom before, if ever, have what Roland Barthes called "the pleasures of the text" been taken this literally—only to be turned upon their heads (65). The sensuality of the reading experience is here, to be sure, but so too is the intimation of the reader's effective suicide through the phallic agency—the killer's dagger—that is an extension of the reader's own complicity. Again as in "Axolotl," the plot line is a line that is looped and reconnected to itself—with a twist: in effect, a Möbius strip; or at least an endless spiral on the Borgesian theme of work-of-art-within-work-of-art.

"The Night Face Up" seems to mean its title to refer to tossing coins; the story is at pains to show the initial character, a motorcycle rider badly injured in a highway accident, as being carried face up to the hospital. There he slips into a recurring dream in which he becomes an Indian being hunted for use as a human sacrifice in some sort of Aztec or Mayan ceremony (Faulkner's "Red Leaves" would seem to have influenced the hunt passages). Cortázar has his injured rider move closer and closer to the moment of his death each time he slips into his "dream"; though he fights his losses of consciousness, he cannot resist the process—which is aided by sensory connections, chiefly of smell. In the end the character knows that the scene of sacrificial death is itself the reality—"he was not going to wake up, that he was awake, that the marvelous dream had been the other, absurd as all dreams are"—and that a priest with a dagger is bringing his death to him where he lies "face up, face up with his eyes closed" (76). The extra twist here is that Cortázar uses the idea of recurring fates in a novel way: his Indian dreams *forward* in time, and the realistic presentation of contemporary surfaces, with which the story begins, yields finally to a fantastic bewilderment. "In the infinite lie of the dream," for instance, the motorcycle blurs into "an enormous metal insect that whirred away between his legs" (76); here an obsessive past consciousness projects itself into futurity, presumably on the strength of (again) imminent and final peril.

In "Bestiary" the obsessive force is the family tensions lurking just behind the actions of the narrative, which are to some extent told from the restricted viewpoint of children—shot from the floor, as it were. Of the animals mentioned in the story, chief among them is the tiger whose presence on the grounds and in the house is mentioned casually on the story's second page (79). If the tiger corresponds to the resentments which are apt to break out in the form of violence (the terror of the tiger is as important an image for Borges as for Blake), the child's perspective is paralleled by the ant farm which occupies the child's attention; to Isabel, "it gave her immense pleasure to think that the ants came and went without fear of any tiger" (85). The pattern by which family stability is maintained on the basis of knowing the whereabouts of the tiger is broken suddenly at the story's end when the Kid, having been told that the tiger is in his study, finds to his fatal dismay that the beast is actually in the library (95). In the final tableau, the character Rema is seen soothing an upset child with "a murmuring against her ear, a stuttering as of gratitude, as of an unnameable acquiescence" (96). Much of the story's power comes from Cortázar's restriction of point of view, which forces upon the reader the need to keep track of the "tiger."

Yet it would be naive to ask whether there is a "real" tiger in "Bestiary," and just as naive to wonder if the dead Celina really comes back to life on the strength of two men's love for her in "The Gates of Heaven," which is next. The narrator has for some time past been occupying himself with a lower-class couple, Celina and Mauro; he refers to Mauro's "simplicity" (100) as well as that of Celina, and reveals that he has been collecting "data" on the latter (101). Finally, with a patent parallel established between his action and Dante's quest for Beatrice ("I was Virgil," he says [105]), he takes Mauro for diversion to a dance hall named the Santa Fe (Celina had been a B-girl before meeting Mauro). Here Cortázar does his best job of rendering for the reader the half-world of the tango-dancing-and-singing nightlife of Buenos Aires. The girls at the Santa Fe, like Celina herself, are short and dark; the speaker calls them "monsters" (108–9). Suddenly both men see Celina in the smoky darkness; though the narrator has painted a picture of hell, it is here that Celina is in "paradise," "heaven," but with the observation that "happiness transfigured her face in a hideous way" (112). The story ends with the narrator pitying Mauro, who has gone off trying to find Celina in the crowd of dancers, not realizing that because he is on "this side" (of death?) he cannot reach her (99, 113). This time the obsessive force is a Holy Faith which transforms a hell into a heaven.

As is obvious in Antonioni's choice of it as a pretext for his film of the same name, "Blow-Up" is one of Cortázar's most ambitious and complex—or densely written—excursions into Borgesian notions of relativity. Michel, his protagonist, is in the business of data-transference; he is by profession a translator, by avocation a photographer. And yet he searches constantly for the right means of telling his story (114), seems to feel both dead and alive (115), and knows that "the photographer always worked as a permutation of his personal way of seeing the world as other than the camera insidiously imposed upon it" (117–18). Yet he is also conscious of the stream of images which he stands in— noting as he does, Hamlet-like, the changing shapes of clouds throughout the story, but being able to let himself "go in the letting go of objects, running immobile in the stream of time" (118). His random searching for images with inherent meaning is handled with suspicion, because Michel knows that "looking oozes with mendacity, because it's that which expels us furthest outside ourselves" (119). When he sees a woman and a young man in a public place and takes their picture, he is able to invent a scenario for the coupling of characters (120–22), but the discovery of a third character distorts his imaginings—he is guilty of "making literature" (124). Yet Michel is constantly distracted by the wind in the leaves, and his sentences go on and on, as if uncertain of their own proper phrasings. An especially interesting moment is the one when Michel becomes aware of the blond woman's eyes— having already rejected his own trial descriptions of her as "unfair"; her eyes, he suggests, fall upon objects "like two eagles, two leaps into nothingness, two puffs of green slime." Rejecting mere description in behalf of understanding, he repeats, "And I said two puffs of green slime" (120). The point of all this is not, in fact, the appropriateness of an image which is echoed elsewhere in the story; it is Michel's stated intent to fix an image—a "meaning"—by force of personal fiat, to work his associations upon the universe. (One thinks of William Carlos Williams' insistent ending to "Portrait of a Lady": "I said petals from an appletree.") The achieved image, itself redolent of his own set of associations, now comes to play itself out for Michel "all at once" (128–29); the scene he has ostensibly interrupted now completes itself before his hypnotized gaze. Like the speaker and like Mauro in "The Gates of Heaven," Michel finds himself "on this side, prisoner of another time" (130). And like the Kid in "Bestiary," his encounter with obsessiveness ends with a scream, as he acknowledges the autonomy of the supposedly "frozen" image (130). The scene incipient in the image on Michel's film plays itself out nevertheless—has its way with Michel—and leaves behind it an empty surface where had been the blow-up of the original "captured" moment. Michel is left with the grey blotches of clouds, pigeons, and raindrops. The creative imagination at work in the most suspect of art forms—the one in which the "creator" seems to count for least—is in the end exhausted by the potentialities of his supposedly subject observances.

The book's third section begins with the volume's title story, "End of the Game." We are concerned here with a trio of children who have established a kind of static theatre of poses and expressions for the benefit of passengers passing by their house by rail. Here Cortázar is at his most elusive: one of the children, Letitia, older and brighter than the rest, is also very ill. Their "game" attracts the attention of one of the passengers, who calls himself "Ariel" and sends a note expressing the wish to meet Letitia. But Letitia does not appear at the arranged meeting, and sends instead a note, the contents of which we never learn. She does, however, provide a last spectacle, one involving both regal bearing and also great physical strain. If it is indeed a pose of renunciation, is it based on what she may have told the boy about her condition? Or did she react according to her class in rejecting a boy who goes, not to the presumably exclusive English school, but to an ordinary trade school? Or has she—a combination of both of the above—used the excuse of class to obscure the real reason she severs their remote relationship? Whatever the answer, Cortázar deliberately blurs the reader's perceptions by again limiting them to what a child might observe. In effect, the collection's title story is one of its most intriguing puzzles! Why "Ariel," of all names, for instance—unless to underscore the hapless physicality of Letitia's condition? We shall not know: the obsessional consciousness breaks off its contact before projection can occur.

Indeed, this last section of longer fictions seems designed to lull us into the expectation that Cortázar has surrendered at last to the naturalistic, has reformed and expressed the desire to lead a conventional, creative life. Not so, even though "At Your Service" can be considered merely a touching depiction of the texture of life experienced by the aged servant Francinet. Given a night's work watching her mistress' pampered dogs during a house party, Francinet completes her chores even though, fatigued, she feels as if she's dreaming—a note echoed elsewhere in the story. Her work ended, she is befriended by a young man in white whose name, she is not unsettled to learn, is Bébé. Later, she is asked by the husband of the first employer to pose as the mother of a recently dead friend whose death took place " 'under very particular circumstances' " (169). She accepts and, on learning that the dead man is none other than Bébé, plays her role to perfection, her grief at the loss of her brief benefactor being apparently quite genuine. She does so in spite of the fact that the attendants at Bébé's wake include men known as Loulou and Nina, who quarrel with a "shriek" (175), and a mysterious man in a scarf who insists on staying near the corpse; and in spite of the fact that her employer, M. Rosay, has been said to be about to take over the firm of fashion design formerly run by Bébé. Francinet's concluding sentiments about everyone's loving poor Bébé can only arouse reader incomprehension at her unwillingness not to *suspect*. But we are not told the purposes behind the charade of Bébé's funeral, nor are our "answers" more than further questionings—as in "End of the Game." One finds oneself recapitulating, rather than criticizing or interpreting, the materials of these two stories; in them, Cortázar has superbly manipulated the stock techniques of the most banal popular fiction to serve his own fantastic purposes. Their revelations are the lack of revelations. We are made victims of our own obsessive and projective intelligences desperately wanting solutions in a fictional world which all too faithfully mirrors our own—"unrealistically."

"The Pursuer" presents us with the image of an artist-creator: a jazz musician named Johnny Carter who is obsessed with time. Indeed, his notions of rationalizing time through his art can be compared to Ralph Ellison's unnamed protagonist (in *Invisible Man*) and his attempts to achieve a sense of identity and to assert it through the making of music out of blackness and through the manipulation of his opponents' sense of time. Yet Johnny's flight from the conventional, fraught with racial considerations as it is, might also remind us (to our critical unease) of another character with the same initials: Faulkner's Joe Christmas from *Light in August*. (It is small consolation to note that Julio Cortázar's initials are also the same.) In any event, "The Pursuer" must stand on its own as one of the finest stories ever written about the world of jazz. (*Benny* Carter is alluded to in an earlier story in the collection.) But one doesn't learn at once that Johnny is black—not until his mania about time is established.

That mania takes unusual forms of expression: for instance, there is the report of a rehearsal session with Miles Davis at which Johnny grows violent at the thought that " 'I already played this tormorrow . . .' " (186). Contradictorily, he explains that while " 'Music got me out of time' " (188), it also " 'put me *into* time' " (189). Johnny believes in time's elasticity, and spells out his notions of a relativistic temporal dimension in imagery which, derived from experiences of riding the metro, confuses his listeners but must strike the reader as Einsteinian (190–91, 193–95). All this is being told by a narrator who is simultaneously writing about Johnny and trying to arrive at an on-paper statement of what Johnny Carter is really like. That narrator is aware of the Christ-ness of Johnny's posture (he alludes half-humorously to a "cross" for Johnny [230]), yet he also diminishes him by pointing out Johnny's lack of "greatness" (224); his flawed conception of Johnny's nature may be at its most accurate when he defines Johnny as "alone up against that [*sic*] he was pursuing, against what was trying to escape him while he was chasing it" (221). That is to say—noting as we must the allusion to the story's title here—that essentially Johnny is being pursued by what he himself is in pursuit of. If that is indeed *himself*, we have launched out on yet another of Cortázar's Möbius strips of time.

The narrator Bruno, Johnny's biographer, is similarly in pursuit of Johnny, desiring to fix him in time in his book and with his limited insight into Johnny's nature. "Sure, there are moments when I wish he were already dead," he admits (236), telegraphing not only the certainty of Johnny's early demise but also revealing his own impatience with his subject's mutability. For Johnny, who has citicized the short-comings of Bruno's book, music has meant the brief possibility that " 'for a while there wasn't anything but always' " (241); for Bruno, it is a relief to be able to have Johnny safely fixed in the second edition of his biography. At the end, Johnny is where he has chased himself;

he has long been haunted by the image of fields full of urns, and urns full of ashes of the dead (210, 213). (One thinks again of how Faulkner's Joe Christmas was haunted by images of urns with a different sort of contents.) Reportedly, Johnny's last words are the beginning of Dylan Thomas' "O Make Me a Mask"—a wish to hide from distorting and inquisitive others—but the people around him, and perhaps even Bruno, do not understand (247). "The Pursuer" tells of the obsessive imagination fixed upon itself and confounded by the effort to escape the self.

In the final story, "Secret Weapons," Cortázar would seem to be writing more "typically." Pierre, a character who speaks a great deal about particularity and who denies the gratuitous (248–49, 251), goes away for a holiday with his girlfriend Michèle—goaded by the notion that he can remember the surroundings in which she grew up, the place they are to visit together. The details which keep returning to his imagination are a glass ball at the bottom of a banister and dry leaves which irritate him by their misplaced presences. Pierre keeps drifting out of himself on the strength of these images, but it is at first as though he is projecting his and Michèle's adventure together. In the end, it turns out that the glass ball belongs to a house Michèle had lived in at an earlier time when—we learn this as the story ends, with violence against Pierre again imminent—she had been attacked by a German soldier whom her friends had executed in the woods. This imminence follows directly upon a scene of Pierre assaulting Michèle, looking to her to be someone else as he does so. The leaves are those of the spot where the German soldier's body had fallen, his bloody face sticking to them as it did so. But with the grown Michèle apparently unable to remember the earlier encounter, the reader is left with the presumption that Pierre has been overtaken by a projection of a more powerful imagination from out of the past: that his death, if it comes, will be a second slaying (cf. "The Night Face Up") of an imaginative and creative force too strong to disappear. Or, putting it more conventionally, that through a loop in time the past had returned to imprint itself upon the present (with a last reference to Faulkner, we recall his denial of the pastness of the past; but the Borgesian version of this notion is even stronger here). *End of the Game* ends as it began, with a transformation and with a surrendering.

In the fictions of Julio Cortázar, the fantastic breaks through masks of the "real" through holes in time—whereas in Borges, they do through magic holes in space—"Alephs," as he chooses to borrow the term for them in one notable story. What surges through such holes in time are, I think, what can be called projections of obsessive consciousness, usually of the creative or imaginative sort, but generally stronger than the realtively-closer-to-a-vacuum sort they may encounter as obstacles in their paths. In doing so, they may make victims of themselves. In Cortázar, there are such things as looking glasses of temporality, and as black holes in time. In each of his fictions, there is a point on which the narrative depends, or is seen to lean upon—some point at which a transformation has astonishingly taken place, or is just about to. At points like these, "subject" becomes "procedure," and content form. Derivative, he is also breathtakingly fresh. He shows us persons who know less than they are confident they do, and in the process educates us as to how much less we know as well. And he guides us into purgatories of the human heart where floods of errant blood rush by—though willy-nilly—all the time.

Evelyn Picon Garfield

It took me many months to read *Octaedro*, mainly because the book distressed me and I had to abandon it several times. When I finally finished reading this last collection of short stories written by Julio Cortázar, I was disturbed by my reaction to the book, for Cortázar had communicated his despair to me in those pages. In many ways these eight short stories seemed to be a continuation of his other works; nevertheless, an indefinable difference existed. These new stories echo the Cortázar with whom I am familiar. In "Verano" (Summertime) a couple's daily routine is interrupted by an unexpected threat; in "Liliana llorando" (Liliana Weeping) and "Los pasos en las huellas" (Footsteps in the Tracks) a hidden dimension of everyday reality is discovered and accepted by the protagonists; in "Manuscrito hallado en un bolsillo" (Manuscript Found in a Pocket) there is a game of chance; in "Lugar llamado Kindberg" (A Place Called Kindberg) and "Cuello de gatito negro" (Neck of the Little Black Cat) there are fortuitous encounters; in "Las fases de Severo" (The Phases of Severo) the strange atmosphere of the story reminds us of the family that lived on Humboldt Street in *Historias de cronopios y de famas* (1962); and finally, obsessive visions of hands and of dreams that haunt one's vigilant hours are found in "Cuello de gatito negro" and "Ahí pero dónde, cómo" (Over There But Where, How). However, in spite of all that was familiar to me in these stories, I could sense an important difference that was difficult to define at first and that I propose to uncover and explain here.

In Cortázar's short stories we expect to encounter a multifaceted reality. By depicting a normal setting and conventional characters Cortázar gains our confidence and puts us at ease with his tales. Innocently reading on, we suddenly find ourselves trapped by a strange and sometimes unreal situation, an oneiric and even fantastic turn of events. In

"*Octaedro*: Eight Phases of Despair," from *The Final Island: The Fiction of Julio Cortázar*, edited by Jaime Alazraki and Ivar Ivask. Copyright © 1976, 1978 by the University of Oklahoma Press.

this way we are exposed to and at times threatened by another possible but illogical dimension of the apparently routine reality set forth in the stories. From "Casa tomada" (The House Taken Over) and "Lejana" (The Distances) in *Bestiario* (1951) to "El otro cielo" (The Other Heaven) in *Todos los fuegos el fuego* (1966) Cortázar has presented us with a view of reality riddled with holes, what I like to call a "Swiss cheese" reality.[1] One of his most famous characters, Johnny of "El perseguidor" (The Pursuer) describes this reality:

> "That made me jumpy, Bruno, *that they felt sure of themselves.* Sure of what, tell me what now, when a poor devil like me with more plagues than the devil under his skin had enough awareness to feel that everything was like a jelly, that everything was very shaky everywhere, you only had to concentrate a little, feel a little, be quiet for a little bit, to find the holes. In the door, in the bed: holes. In the hand, in the newspaper, in time, in the air: everything full of holes, everything spongy, like a colander straining itself . . ."[2]

Through those same holes the unexplained danger of "Casa tomada" filters throughout the house. In that story a strange noise takes over the rooms and forces the sister and brother to abandon their home. In "Lejana" of the same collection (*Bestiario*), by means of a "sponge-like" reality, the protagonist Alina Reyes establishes a strange psychic relationship with an old beggar-woman in Budapest. She dreams about her and finally feels compelled to travel to Budapest to seek her out. When the two women meet on the bridge and embrace, a surprising transmigration of souls occurs. "Alina's soul lodges in the beggar-woman's body while the beggar-woman's soul takes over Alina's body and so the beggar-woman is really the victorious one."[3] In that way Alina's dream world overtakes her everyday existence in a completely illogical way, contrary to our laws of space and time.

In a more recent take, "El otro cielo," the "colander-reality" serves as a passageway for the protagonist to partake of two lives in distinct places and epochs: twentieth-century Argentina and Paris in the 1870s. Unlike "Casa tomada" and "Lejana," where the characters succumb to a facet of reality which they either imagine or dream, in "El otro cielo" the protagonist finally abandons his exciting life in the Paris of bygone days to return to a routine existence in Buenos Aires. Hardly a threat, Parisian life was a coveted adventure which materialized by means of the protagonist's desire but which ultimately vanished forever.

Part 3

In the newest collection, *Octaedro*, we once again glimpse the daily existence of a couple as they are threatened by inexplicable forces in the form of a little girl and a mysterious white horse. The setting of the short story "Verano" is clearly autobiographical—the house, "the path full of ruts and loose stones," the hills, the swallows, the flight from the capital to a countryside which evokes Saignon, where Cortázar spends his summers. Whereas in "Casa tomada" the brother narrates the life which he and his sister lead and thus allows us to share directly in the couple's most trivial pastimes, in "Verano" the third-person narrator observes and comments on Zulma and Mariano's life together. Their routine existence is filled with "nimias delicadas ceremonias convencionales" in the country during the summertime as well as in the city during the rest of the year: "It was all coming full circle again, everything in time and a time for everything, except for the girl who suddenly and gently unhinged the scheme."[4] Cortázar's sentiments about the routine nature of existence surface again here as they did in previous works: *Historias de cronopios y de famas* (1962), *Rayuela* (1963), *La vuelta al día en ochenta mundos* (1967) and *Ultimo round* (1969). In those books the author alluded to domesticated life and custom in pejorative terms, describing them as a nightmare, an absurdity and as "un lugar donde estamos muertos."[5] Ever since *Las armas secretas* (1958) the exceptional departures from routine life and the glimpses of an illogical and provocative facet of everyday reality seem to have become gradually surpressed by the heavy and relentless hand of custom. Routine seems to reestablish itself more and more in Cortázar's stories, despite the author's clear protests in his volumes of miscellaneous excerpts. Even in "El perseguidor" the jazz critic Bruno sought refuge in his customary life in order to protect himself from the provocative reality that Johnny perceived and described through is music. Neither did the protagonist of "El otro cielo" return to the mysterious galleries of Paris, but instead he remained in Buenos Aires, subjected to a conventional life.

Of all the stories published before *Octaedro*, "La autopista del sur" (The Southern Thruway) best exemplifies the definitive victory of routine over a desired and exceptional reality. In that story Cortázar is true to his view of the fantastic as "la alteración momentánea dentro de la regularidad."[6] In "La autopista del sur" some travelers find themselves immobilized in a traffic jam. This common situation achieves unrealistic proportions when the traffic jam lasts months. As the seaons rapidly progress, the people organize a societal nucleus among the stationary cars and eventually embrace a new routine as inhabitants of the highway, until suddenly the cars once again begin to move toward the capital. Even in the face of a fantastic and bizarre situation such as a traffic jam which lasts months, custom reestablishes its sovereignty.

Whereas in "La autopista del sur" the narrative prose communicates a rhythm of routine existence and of implacable time, in "Verano" the narration is more in the nature of a commentary about the weariness of existence between man and woman. Zulma and Mariano's "ready-made" life together is described in the following manner: "One more month of expected repetitions, as if rehearsed, and the jeep loaded to the brim would take them back to the apartment in the capital, to the life that was identical but for its visible gestures" (79). This mild protest against custom and the realization of all that is humdrum in the coexistence of man and woman has a counterpoint in the story. Zulma reminds Mariano that he too has his own routine obsessions—for instance, he always places his bottle of cologne on the left and his razor on the right. It is precisely at that moment that Mariano admits that custom has a reason for being: "But they weren't manias, Mariano thought, but more like a defense against death and nothingness, to order things and hours, to establish rites and passages against a confusion filled with holes and stains" (81). To Mariano custom is a defense against the unknown, whereas for the musician Johnny of "El perseguidor" custom was hateful. His critic Bruno was attracted to the vision of another mysterious and exceptional facet of reality that Johnny seemed capable of experiencing through his music, but Bruno also sensed a protective order in his own routine life. On the other hand, Mariano reaches beyond Bruno's intuition of a protective routine to justify custom, to accept tradition and to defend daily habit. The mild protests which Mariano expresses against humdrum life and his defense of custom as a weapon against death and nothingness seem very different and distant from the protest made by Cortázar in the following passage about another jazz musician, Clifford Brown, in *La vuelta al día* (p. 73): "And afterward routine returns, where he and so many more of us are dead."

In "Verano" Zulma and Mariano's tranquil existence is interrupted when a friend leaves his little girl with them overnight and during that same night a white horse tries to break into the house. An interesting comparison can be made between the threat to this couple's house and life and similar dangers in the first stories of *Bestiario*. In "Casa tomada," a story which was motivated by a nightmare that Cortázar had, a threateningly mysterious noise invades the house from within and forces the couple to abandon it. In another tale, "Cefalea" (from *Bestiario*), Cortázar describes the migraine headaches that plagued him. The *mancuspias* in "Cefalea" are strange animals which surround the house in which their caretakers live. Actually, the house and the caretakers' minds, both besieged by the animals, are synonymous. Above all, the dual menace of the girl and the horse in "Verano" recalls the situation found in the title story of the first collection, "Bestiario." That story was the result of a hallucination that Cortázar experienced when he was ill with an extreme fever. In the story a young girl, Isabel, who is visiting her relatives, the Funes family, becames accustomed to the presence of a tiger that roams at will through the rooms. The family has devised a system of warnings so that no one will enter the particular room wher the tiger happens to be. Isabel is very fond of her Aunt Rema and consequently senses that Rema's brother-in-law Nene is cruel to her. As if Isabel controlled the dangerous animal, she lies to Nene concerning the tiger's whereabouts, with the result that Nene enters the library and is attacked by the animal.

In "Verano" Zulma discerns a strange complicity between the girl who is visiting them for the night and the horse crashing against the window, a liaison which had been developed earlier between Isabel and the tiger in "Bestiario." Zulma insists that the girl will open the door to let the horse in, and, in fact, the next morning the door to the garden is wide open. Unlike the disquieting invasions found in the short stories of *Bestiario*, in "Verano" the unusual provocation to daily routine materializes in the form of a horse, a less oneiric danger than an inexplicable noise, a less fantastic threat than some fabulous *mancuspias* and a more realistic intrusion than that of a tiger roaming through a house. In addition, the ephemeral presence of the horse and child does not threaten to destroy permanently the couple's ordered daily coexistence. In fact, at the end of the story a long sentence rhythmically embodies the implacable return of routine:

> . . . if everything was in order, if the watch kept on measuring the morning and after Florencio came to get the little girl perhaps around 12 o'clock the mailman would arrive whistling from afar, leaving the letters on the garden table where he or Zulma would pick them up silently, just before deciding together what they felt like having for lunch. (90)

We still have to ask Cortázar about the genesis of this story. As with those in *Bestiario*, is it the result of a nightmare, a hallucination, a headache caused by a particularly difficult period in his life? What is the significance of Zulma's terrified reaction to the child and the horse? One critic suggests that Zulma fears Mariano's erotic advances, which she has been avoiding all summer.[7] This is an interesting interpretation which would certainly have a precedent in the short story "El río" (The River). Other critics have viewed her horror as a result of the couple's lack of communication, for the white horse symbolizes and illuminates the estranged relationship between man and woman.[8] Neither of these interpretations attributes enough importance to the role of the young girl, a role which I consider to be fundamental to understanding the story. She is an intruder whose childlike innocence is echoed in the whiteness of the horse and who may represent the daughter that Zulma does not have or does not want to have, a child whose presence would upset the tranquil albeit stagnant life that the couple leads.

Keeping in mind the extreme reaction of fear that Zulma experiences because of the dual presence of the girl and the animal, let us suggest still another rendering based on the traditional sexual symbolism of the horse and the specific eroticism which one encounters in other girls and, by extension, in dolls, that appear in Cortázar's works such as "Silvia," "Siestas" and "La muñeca rota" (The Broken Doll) in *Ultimo round*, and in the novel *62: Modelo para armar*. Perhaps the young girl is an intruder in the established liaison between man and woman, or perhaps she acts as a catalyst by awakening the dormant erotic conjugal relationship. The young girl completes a triangle necessary to the recovery of lost eroticism, an eroticism which always psosesses a certain amount of sadism, according to Cortázar—that is, the terror that Zulma feels. In the tradition of his previous stories, Cortázar encourages us to interpret "Verano" in many different ways. On the other hand, unlike the characters in his earlier stories, Zulma and Mariano seem to have become more accustomed to the involuntary intrusions upon their lives. Rather than abandon routine existence, they quickly recover from the mysterious invasion and, with the toothpaste of the following morning's routine, calmly plug up the holes communicating with the exceptionally provocative event of the previous night.

Despite the persistence of routine, dreams, obsessions and imagination prevail in *Octaedro*—with a notable difference. In these stories Cortázar speaks more directly to the reader. He is not content to suggest that there is another side to apparent reality, for he not only imagines and dreams about "otherness" but also takes pains to define that exceptional zone for us. In the story "Liliana llorando" a young man who is fatally ill tries to keep the news from his wife. In order to forget his pain, he keeps a diary of his thoughts and assures the reader that he can "think about anything at all as long as I can write it down immediately" (10). Like the protagonist, Cortázar himself has written stories and even novels to exorcise the obsessions created by his imagination. While the protagonist envisions the sadness his wife will feel when he dies, he plots his own despair, for he dreams of his wife's being consoled by Alfred, a family friend. Near the end of the story, although the patient seems to be regaining his health, he still intends to keep Liliana from knowing of his recovery, for in his dreams she is happy in the arms of another. His dreams have become reality.

Cortázar often develops an interesting relationship between scientific women and the men they betray. One should remember the painful relationship between the adolescent boy and the nurse in "La señorita Cora" (Nurse Cora) and between the anesthetist Hélène and Juan, or his double the dead boy, in *62*. One day Cortázar mentioned to me that certain sadomasochistic attractions exist for him in these relationships between male patients and the women who care for them and at times cause them much pain. Liliana, in this new story, is a chemist, and although she does not directly take care of her husband, in his imagination and finally in reality she deceives him. The protagonist in "Liliana llorando" creates his own reality and transcribes it. Unlike Cortázar, who wrote down his nightmares and obsessions in the short stories of *Bestiario* in order to free himself of them, the patient in this story does not achieve the same exorcism. Instead of ridding himself of these obsessive thoughts, he establishes them as a clear truth which he finally accepts.

Even more painful is the situation of the narrator in "Ahí pero dónde, cómo." In that story Cortázar himself is the protagonist who shares with the reader a recurrent dream about the death of his friend Paco. Throughout the story Cortázar relives the last days before Paco's death in an incessant succession of painfully realistic scenes. In previous stories like "La noche boca arriba" (The Night Face Up) or "El río" the protagonist's dreams persist in and even fuse with wakefulness at the end of each tale. On the other hand, "Ahí pero dónde, cómo" is hardly a short story, but rather an attempt on Cortázar's part to isolate the illogical sensation of dream-wakefulness, to contemplate himself in this agonizing state and to communicate it to us by means of the printed page. In an earlier story, "Las babas del diablo" (translated as "Blow-Up"), the protagonist Michel struggled to describe a difficult situation in his life. Now Cortázar proposes to recount the persistence of a dream that is more real to him than the phenomenological reality that surrounds him. Cortázar once told me of a similar situation: "It's one thing to have an abstract idea that doesn't penetrate your veins, your marrow, but there are those ideas that are almost hallucinatory, that torment you because they are made of flesh and blood, they are more real than the other ideas." Cortázar urges us to recall similar experiences so that he need not feel so alone while he tries in vain to communicate his own anguish to us:

> I probably haven't been able to make you feel that way, but I'm writing it anyhow for you who are reading me because it's a way of breaking the cycle, of asking that you search within yourself to see if you, too, have one of those cats, one of those who are dead, whom you loved and who are over there in a place that I am desperately trying to name with paper words. (105)

The story is clearly autobiographical—Geneva, translators, Chile— to the extent that the author winks at us when he says, "And you the reader probably think that I'm inventing all this; so what, for a long time now people have been calling imaginary those events that I've really lived, and vice versa" (104). Actually, in the story there are many references to his other books. He alludes to *62* and to the city that he writes about in that novel, a city that he has dreamt about since he was twenty years old. Although he wrote a poem and then an entire novel in order to exorcise that nightmare, Cortázar still dreams of that strange city. He described it to me in this way: "When I wrote the poem, I thought, all right, this is an exorcism, I'm not going to dream about the city again; but when I finished it, a few weeks later, I went down there again and I've gone down there several times since." Nevertheless in "Ahí pero dónde, cómo" he informs us that the recurrent dream about Paco has nothing to do with his dream of the city; Paco is another matter entirely. As in previous works, Cortázar's predilection for surrealist painters[9] continues in the dedication to this story, where he names René Magritte's famous painting of a pipe ironically entitled "Esto no es una pipa." During our interview, as Cortázar described his enthusiasm for surrealist paintings, he referred to that very painting:

> If you look at a Matisse you don't need to find any story behind it, only plastic values count; the same with a Braque or a Jackson Pollock. On the other hand, you can't look at a Dalí or a Magritte without knowing what it's called because even though the title has no apparent connection with the painting, it does have something to do with it. When Magritte, I don't know if it is Magritte or Man Ray, paints a huge pipe and calls the painting "This is not a pipe," there is an entire system of thought and metaphor that comes into play there.

In a similar fashion by means of the short story Cortázar tries to make us share an experience which logic tells us is only a recurrent dream but which Cortázar knows is more real than reality itself. Like Magritte, he assures us, "Esto no es un sueño."

Even when dreams and fecund imagination do not openly and defiantly subvert apparent reality, Cortázar insists on revealing the hypocritical acceptance of a false reality to which man so readily succumbs. In his works pursuers such as Johnny and Oliveira recognize the spurious nature of the lives they lead, while other characters such as Madame Francinet in "Los buenos servicios" (At Your Service) never identify more than the surface reality of a complex situation. In *Octaedro* this theme is dealt with in "Los pasos en las huellas" when the critic Fraga thinks that he is writing the poet Romero's true biography. It is not long before Fraga realizes that he has hypocritically chosen to emphasize the poet's greatness while ignoring his baseness. In order to achieve fame, Fraga has created his own selective biography. Realizing his complicity in support of a legend about the poet, Fraga decides to expose the false myth and, consequently, his own hypocrisy. The critic Bruno in the story "El perseguidor" also infuses his book about Johnny's music with his own feelings and thoughts about jazz. He falsifies the soul of Johnny's music, and the musician berates him on that account. Unlike Bruno, Fraga realizes his error, recognizes the infamous side of the poet's nature and intends to make his discovery public, thus risking his own career.

If one takes as a point of departure "Los pasos en las huellas" and "Liliana llorando," it is possible to see that *Octaedro* is also concerned with the process of writing, a preoccupation which first appeared as a theme in the stories of *Las armas secretas*. Aside from the reference to Poe's story "MS Found in a Bottle," the title "Manuscrito hallado en un bolsillo" reminds us of Cortázar's own manuscripts which he had misplaced, later found and finally published as "El perseguidor" and "Estación de la mano" (Season of the Hand). In "Manuscrito hallado en un bolsillo" Cortázar once again demonstrates his predilection for games of chance. The story reminds us of the graffiti found on the walls of the University in Paris, a message which Cortázar reprinted for us in "Noticias del mes de mayo" (News for the Month of May; *Ultimo round*). The ironic explanation proclaims the following: "HAY QUE EXPLORAR SISTEMATICAMENTE EL AZAR"—"One must systematically explore chance." And that is precisely what the protagonist in "Manuscrito hallado en un bolsillo" does. He takes the subway and adheres to an itinerary, all the while hoping that some other passenger's travel plans will coincide with his own: "That was the rule of the game, a smile reflected in the window and the right to follow a woman and desperately hope that her next move would coincide with the one that I had decided on before the trip began" (62). The protagonist dictates the rules of the game in which Marie-Claude finally participates. This underground search differs considerably from Cortázar's earlier games in that it is not as dangerous nor as metaphysical nor even as humorous as the games that La Maga and Oliveira used to play in *Rayuela*. In spite of the possible existential interpretation of man's life as a journey fraught with chance encounters, the protagonist's adventure lacks the requisite anguish and in fact seems to be more a gratuitous pastime, despite the story's last suspense-filled moments.

In this story, as in "Lugar llamado Kindberg" and "Cuello de gatito negro," Cortázar continues to be fascinated with trains and railroad schedules as well as with fortuitous encounters, a predilection manifest in his novels *Los premios* and *62*. In these three new short stories chance meetings form the focal point of the plots. During our interview Cortázar spoke to me of water as a symbolic element of communication between individuals and of bridges and trains:

> You know that I have other places for rites of passage and I don't think they're very Jungian. For example, streetcars or trains obsess me terribly. . . . It's sort of like a projection of the bridge idea. A streetcar or a train is a bridge that moves, besides they frequently pass over actual bridges. But inside, they themselves are a "no-man's land," because streetcars and buses are strange. In them a

bunch of people who don't know each other are thrown together and are moved along in space and time. This creates a kind of unity separated from all else. Then that situation seems to me to be able to determine the function of certain unknown laws; certain things can happen there that do not occur outside.

The idea of "figures" has intrigued Cortázar for quite some time now. He gave Luis Harss the following explanation: "I'm constantly sensing the possibility of certain links, of circuits that close around us, interconnecting us in a way that defies all rational explanation and has nothing to do with the ordinary human bonds that join people."[10] In the novel *Los premios* Persio is the first to mention the concept of figures, and later Cortázar himself was to describe accidental coincidences that occurred in his own life and works in "De otra máquina célibe" (Of Another Celibate Machine) and "Encuentros a deshora" (Inopportune Encounters) from *La vuelta al día* and in "Marcela del campo o más encuentros a deshora" and "La muñeca rota" from *Ultimo round*. Many of his short stories such as "La noche boca arriba," "Las armas secretas" and "Todos los fuegos el fuego" (All Fires the Fire) and his novel *Rayuela* also reveal these seemingly fortuitous bonds between people, places and events. In fact, Cortázar creates an entire novel, *62: Modelo para armar*, based on a great web of destinies in which characters' paths cross by chance in a series of accidental and purposeful meetings, which when viewed in their totality must represent a "figure."[11] Each character forms a star in a vast constellation unknown to him.

In the three short stories under discussion—"Manuscrito hallado en un bolsillo," "Cuello de gatito negro" and "Lugar llamado Kindberg"—the man who is traveling in the subway or on the highway meets a woman by chance. At the end of each story there is always a definitive break in the very short-lived relationship between man and woman. In fact, with the conclusion of each story the man faces death as a fact or as an implied presence, whereas the woman continues on her way. These women are always described in paternalistic terms as little girls or small animals, especially when they are crying, and they almost always have occasion to weep. When she discovers that she is a coparticipant in a game of chance, Marie-Claude cries "like a wounded little animal" in "Manuscrito hallado en un bolsillo"; the mulatto Dina in "Cuello de gatito negro" is "crying, mewing like a wounded cat"; and the young hitchhiker Lina in "Lugar llamado Kindberg" is described as a "childlike little bear cub" and a "girl-scout cub." One could refer to other women in these stories: Liliana, who weeps a lot, is also described as having "slow feline movements," and she smiles "almost like a little girl"; Severo's wife cries in "Las fases de Severo"; and Fraga's lover Ofelia weeps silently in "Los pasos en las huellas." Incidentally, in "Manuscrito hallado en un bolsillo" and "Los pasos en las huellas" Cortázar uses his sister's name for the first time in his short stories and perhaps in his entire works. Another critic once pointed out the incestuous relationship between brother and sister in the short story "Casa tomada." Many years ago Cortázar mentioned this interpretation to me and then spoke of his sister Ofelia:

> I have only one sister. What's curious is that on a conscious level my sister and I have nothing in common. We've never understood each other. We're like night and day; we've even come to hate each other. Now with time, since we don't see each other, a more cordial relationship exists. But there's a great difference between us. Nevertheless in dreams many times I've awakened astounded because I've gone to bed with my sister in my dreams.

These three short stories and the three female characters in them echo familiar themes and types in Cortázar's works. In "Manuscrito hallado en un bolsillo" the protagonist desires Marie-Claude as if she were "an end, like the truly final stop of the last subway of life" (70). This statement recalls Oliveira's desire in *Rayuela* that love be a key to the absolute: "a passport-love, a mountain pass-love, a key-love, a revolver-love."[12] In the short story woman and love are still viewed as bridges to total being: "the possibility that everything would coincide at once" (62).

In "Cuello de gatito negro" Cortázar juxtaposes his "totemic" animal, the cat, and his constant obsession with hands. In this story the mulatto Dina finds herself compelled to touch and play with strangers' hands in the subway. That is precisely the way in which she meets the protagonist of the story, who accompanies her home. The plot reaches its peak in a terrifying scene of passion when Dina uncontrollably scratches her lover as if she were a cat and he defends himself by seizing her by the neck. Well before *Octaedro*, in the story "No se culpa a nadie" (Don't You Blame Anyone), Cortázar had described a hand which attacked its owner as he attempted to put on a blue pullover sweater. When I asked the author why he and some of his most famous characters such as Oliveira of *Rayuela* and Juan of *62* were so interested in hands, he spoke of his obsession:

> Hands have always obsessed me since I was very young. In the first things I wrote, hands played a very important role. I was very young when I wrote that text which I later put into *Ultimo round*, the one that's called "The Season of the Hand." It's the story of a man who sees a hand enter the house, walk around and become his friend. Until one day the hand senses that the man is afraid of it, and then it leaves and never returns. I have an obsession that is somewhat morbid. You know, when I'm alone at home and there's a pair of gloves, mine or someone else's, men's or women's, on top of a table, I never go to sleep without putting them in a drawer or placing some heavy object on top of them, because I'm not able to sleep knowing that these gloves have been left alone in the house. I have the feeling that something is going to bring them to life at any moment.

Cortázar spoke to me of childhood traumas occasioned by tales of strangulations and by horror films like *The Hands of Horlack* with Peter Lorre. He then added: "You know that for a somewhat morbid imagination like mine there is a whole cycle of hands that come and go in my books." And so his obsession with hands appears once again in "Cuello de gatito negro."

As in *Libro de Manuel*, in "Lugar llamado Kindberg" the protagonist is attracted to young people—especially to women—who hold "a world view that had perhaps also once been his own" (113). These are Marcelo's thoughts as he observes the hitchhiker Lina. In Cortázar's latest novel, *Libro de Manuel*, there are letters from a hippy named Sara, who reminds us of Lina in "Lugar llamado Kindberg." A very interesting albeit partial interchange of the traditional roles attributed to man and woman occurs in this story. Unlike the independent and unconventional Oliveira or the men in *Libro de Manuel*, the protagonist Marcelo is characterized as a "salesman of prefabricated materials," an inhabitant of a "protective bourgeois bubble." He realizes that Lina belongs to a younger generation and refers to her in jazz terminology (another constant in Cortázar's works): "es una osita Shepp, ya no tango, che" (111). Lina travels along with her possessions in a backpack, the way Cortázar likes to travel, like a snail. One might recall the snail Osvaldo in *62* and the observatories of Jai Singh in *Prosa del observatorio*. Cortázar himself describes his affection for this small animal: "The snail lives the way I like to live, sort of self-sufficiently; he moves through life with all his possessions. He carries along his own house." In the short story Lina reproaches Marcelo for his conventional life. "I never arrange anything, why should I? The backpack is like me and this trip and politics, all mixed together and so what?" (113). As if he were her father, she calls him "doctor y papá" and feels at ease by his side because he has long since experienced much of life. As if embodying a maternalistic counterpoint to Lina's sentiments, this evokes in Marcelo memories of a schoolteacher with whom he had fallen in love at the age of twelve. In this manner their personalities and lives are established and fixed: a man weighed down by the ballast of a traditional and comfortable bourgeois existence, a prefabricated life interrupted once in a while by an amorous adventure, and the liberated young woman who feels comfortably lulled by the presence of the "father" figure.

Another interesting twist to the traditional feminine-masculine role is found in an altered yet familiar image. In this story the well-known metaphor that is usually expressed by a male figure to describe Paris as his lover is replaced by Lina's allusion to Copenhagen: "And I told you I don't want to tie myself down, IdontwanttoIdontwantto, Copenhagen is like a man you meet and leave (ah)" (118). The free-spirited Lina is much more akin to the active character of Ludmilla in *Libro de Manuel* than to the famous and intuitive La Maga in *Rayuela*, although both women serve their men as mere bridges in the desired search for complete experience and a grasp of significant and total reality.[13] Despite their superficially free lives, Ludmilla and Lina are not at all independent and, in fact, are defined in part by their respective desires for Marcos and Marcelo.

There are also some limited parallels between the men, between Andrés in *Libro de Manuel* and Marcelo. The former decides to participate in the kidnapping scheme after much hesitation unknown to other Cortázar heroes like Oliveira, while the latter rejects the continued adventure with Lina. Marcelo met her by chance and saw his own abandoned youth reflected in her: "Love didn't even abolish that mirror reflecting the past, the old portrait of himself as a young man that Lina placed before him" (123). At the end of the story he leaves her and speeds away down the road, where he crashes into a tree "at 160 with his face smashed up against the steering wheel, the way Lina used to lower her head because that's how bear cubs eat sugar" (125). Lina is spontaneous jazz, freedom adrift in the world, love that seeks no ties;

and he is a "corredor de materiales prefabricados," who rejects Lina on his way to death.

Perhaps it is the presence of death and tears that exasperates me as I read *Octaedro*. Nevertheless, death is constantly a part of almost all of Cortázar's works. As he himself pointed out, "death is a very important and omnipresent element in all I have written." Perhaps my reaction to these stories is influenced in part by Cortázar's last novel, *Libro de Manuel*, published a year before *Octaedro*. In that book, as before in *Rayuela*, the author juxtaposes playful and humorous situations with serious ones and adds a new political emphasis. I miss the Homo ludens so apparent in Lonstein's language, in the scenes concerning the strange mushroom, the fantastic turquoise penguins or the absurd protests unleashed in the restaurant. By now, however, I should be quite accustomed to the obvious lack of humor in Cortázar's short stories. Since *Historias de cronopios y de famas*, perhaps his most surrealistic book from the perspective of a playful atmosphere reminiscent of paintings by Joan Miró, the short stories have continued to be devoid of the humor found in the novels. It was, in fact, Calac and Polanco's ridiculous adventures which at moments saved the novel *62* from its abysmal cynicism. Are there any such playful and humorous elements which deliver *Octaedro* from the weary despair and sadness which penetrate every page?

In *Octaedro* there are mere suggestions of the strange mixture of black humor and Alfred Jarry's pataphysics that surround the family living on Humboldt Street in the pages of *Historias de cronopios y de famas*. In "Las fases de Severo" the protagonist-narrator and Severo's other friends and relatives attend a strange ritual in which they observe Severo as he is stricken by a series of involuntary and illogical "phases." Amid drinks and sobs the spectators spend the night watching Severo as if he were the bewitched focus of a "happening," a ritual played out previously; for as the narrator tells us, "that evening everything seemed to happen more quickly" (132).[14] The story describes the successive "phases" that Severo experiences: perspiring, jumping, having his face covered by moths, mysteriously assigning numbers to relatives and friends and finally commanding the spectators to set their watches ahead or back. As Severo passes through his phases like the moon through its own, the atmosphere is filled with the suggestive symbolism of a fantastic albeit possible situation, viewed by sympathetic friends and family. Moving in and out of his bedroom, they converse and drink as if they were engaged in a normal experience, a situation which reminds us of the wake described in *Historias de cronopios y de famas*. Despite the fantastic nature of Severo's "phases," his experiences do not terrify us.

Graciela Coulson and Pedro Lastra offer an interesting biblical interpretation of Severo's phases as a metaphor of the passion and death of man.[15] Despite the originality of this rendering, I prefer to approach the story from a surrealistic perspective for two reasons: first, Cortázar has rarely exhibited interest in Christian symbolism, unless one remembers his brief description of the saxophonist Johnny Carter on his knees like a Christ on the cross; and second, the short story's dedication to a Mexican painter, Remedios Varo, reinforces the author's predilection for those who capture the atmosphere of surrealist art and philosophy, as he has done himself in earlier works, especially in *Historias de cronopios y de famas*, perhaps the best precursor or "Las fases de Severo."

Let us first take as a point of departure a description that Cortázar gave me of surrealist art, and then let us seek correspondences:

> The literary content of surrealist painting, Dalí's, Magritte's, for example, Tanguy's, is obvious. They are paintings that have an exclusively esthetic pictorial value on the one hand, but that also have content, a background of an anecdotal, symbolic, psychoanalytical nature—as in Dalí's case—which is important and which you cannot separate from the painting itself.

In the paintings of Remedios Varo the figures have very similar faces, almost as if they were all the same person in different and strange scenes or phases. Nevertheless, they are always surrounded by normal and realistic objects, as in the story about Severo. The fantastic atmosphere that surrounds Remedios's characters as well as Cortázar's Severo is based on their situation, their fantastic use of everyday reality. Ida Rodriquez Prampolini describes Remedios's paintings in her book entitled *El surrealismo y el arte fantástico de México*. That very description could easily apply to Cortázar's short story "Las fases de Severo":

> The juxtaposition of the real and the fantastic comes about naturally, with obvious "tenderness," with surprising enthusiasm, but it never becomes evil, horrifying. . . . The characters are always busy at marvelous chores. . . . Whenever horror does exist, it provokes curiosity, it is not destructive.[16]

Part 3

There are also similarities between the situation in which Severo, friends and family find themselves and the adventures undertaken by the family on Humboldt Street in *Historias de cronopios y de famas*. However, there is an important difference: all humor has vanished. In "Ocupaciones raras," while the sisters practice howling like wolves, the family builds a scaffold with gallows and a rack in the patio in front of the house, where they finally sit down to dine surrounded by horrified neighbors. In another episode the family takes over the post office, where they give out colored balloons, drinks and snacks along with the stamps. In these anecdotes there is a playful atmosphere of gratuitous absurdity and even black humor which makes us laugh. This is no longer so in "Las fases de Severo," despite the words spoken between the narrator and Severo's child after the last phase:

> —Aren't they playing anymore?—Severo's son asked me, as he was falling asleep but still hanging on with a child's stubbornness.
> —No, now it's time to go to sleep—I told him.—Your mom is going to put you to bed; get inside, it's cold.
> —It was a game. Wasn't it, Jules?
> —Sure, kid, it was a game. Go to bed now. (142)

I should have believed Cortázar when he said that *Historias de cronopios y de famas* is a book which should only be written once. He categorized it as his most playful book, "really a game, a very fascinating game, lots of fun, almost like a tennis match, sort of like that." Then he cautioned me that it was necessary to distinguish between the ingenuous joy of that collection and the humor which he planned to conserve in the rest of his books. Nevertheless, in *Octaedro* he has hardly preserved humor in any form.

Traditionally humor had not played an important role in Cortázar's short stories, nor does it now. Instead, the primary characteristics of his short stories have been the constant threat of an illogical and mysterious force to man in his daily existence and the subsequent defeat of that apparent reality by the unknown. *Octaedro* continues the short story tradition established by Cortázar, for it, too, haunts us with nightmares, obsessions and disconcerting provocations which menace everyday existence. But there is a serious and sad divergence from previous tales. The strange zone which Cortázar continues to describe no longer implacably terrifies nor intrigues the protagonists, nor the reader nor even

Cortázar himself, as much as it produces despair. The author tries to describe this other illogical facet of reality in more realistic terms than was done in previous stories. It seems that the terror once experienced in the face of the unknown has now given way to a compromise won over many years. As Cortázar himself says in "Las fases de Severo": "It is always surprising to see how sudden lapses into normalcy, so to speak, distract and even deceive us" (135).

The different atmospheres that prevail in Cortázar's novels and short stories have become more obvious in these last few years. In the short stories man is as impotent as ever when faced with the exceptional in life, although at times he still seeks it out and plays to discover it. He now more easily accepts fleeting chance encounters and momentary outbursts of terror, after which he almost always returns in despair to accept routine life or to face death. In the novels, on the other hand, the author's joyful imagination fights to survive by means of unusual adventures, ingeniously playful language and political optimism. For instance, despite the descriptions of political torture, *Libro de Manuel* saves Cortázar's fiction from wallowing in the cynicism of the previous novel, *62*. As with *Rayuela*, *Libro de Manuel* embodies possible searches; and in opposition to the pervasive and definitive presence of death at the end of *62*, death in the final scenes of *Libro de Manuel* promises regeneration.

It is important to note that love continues to fail completely in the last two novels, for Juan and his friends in *62* as well as for Andrés in *Libro de Manuel*. Nevertheless, in the latter novel the pessimism generated by the absence of unselfish love between man and woman in the individual, personal sphere is diminished by optimism in the political and ideological sphere. *Octaedro* is very different from that latest novel, for these short stories are laden with death, tears, fleeting love affairs and impossible explanations. The pessimism that prevails on the personal level of love between man and woman is but one element of the human destinies that are ultimately altered very little by exceptional events and discoveries glimpsed through dreams, obsessions, dangerous provocations and even chance. *Octaedro* is a continuation of the Cortázar that we know, but there is a difference: Julio is finally accustomed to viewing the other zone of reality. He knows it is there. He experiences it. He tries to share it with us. But he finally must return from it to his everyday reality in despair.

Part 3

Notes

1. For a discussion of the "other reality" in Cortázar's works see the chapter "Swiss Cheese Reality" in *Julio Cortázar* by Evelyn Picon Garfield, New York, Ungar, 1975, pp. 11–76, and the chapter "La realidad dual" in *¿Es Julio Cortázar un surrealista?* by Evelyn Picon Garfield, Madrid, Gredos, 1975, pp. 13–72.

2. *Blow-Up and Other Stories*, Paul Blackburn, tr., New York, Collier, 1963, pp. 190–91.

3. Unpublished interview with Julio Cortázar by Evelyn Picon Garfield in July 1973. Subsequent personal comments by Cortázar are from this interview unless otherwise noted. The translations are my own.

4. *Octaedro*, Buenos Aires, Sudamericana, 1975, pp. 78–79. Future references to this edition will be made in the text by citing the page number in parentheses directly after the passage. The translations are my own.

5. Respectively: *La vuelta al día en ochenta mundos*, Mexico City, Siglo XXI, 1967, p. 68; *Rayuela*, Buenos Aires, Sudamericana, 1963, p. 197; *La vuelta al día*, p. 73.

6. *Ultimo round*, Mexico City, Siglo XXI, 1969, pp. 44–45.

7. Rosario Ferré, "Ocho caras del miedo," *Zona de carga y descarga*, Puerto Rico, 1975, pp. 11, 31.

8. Pedro Lastra, Graciela Coulson, "El motivo del horror en *Octaedro*," *Nueva narrativa hispanoamericana*, 5 (1975), pp. 7–16.

9. For a discussion of the influence of surrealist art on Cortázar's works see *¿Es Julio Cortázar un surrealista?*

10. Luis Harss, Barbara Dohmann, *Into the Mainstream*, New York, Harper & Row, 1967, p. 227.

11. For a discussion of "figures," chance and magnetic fields in Cortázar's works see *¿Es Julio Cortázar un surrealista?*, pp. 139–44, 167–73.

12. *Hopsctoch*, Gregory Rabassa, tr., New York, Pantheon, 1966, p. 425.

13. For a discussion of "El amor y la mujer" in Cortázar's works see *¿Es Julio Cortázar un surrealista?*, pp. 96–118.

14. For a discussion of the "happening" in Cortázar's works see *¿Es Julio Cortázar un surrealista?*, pp. 154–61.

15. "El motivo del horror en *Octaedro*," pp. 13–14.

16. Mexico City, Instituto de Investigaciones Estéticas, 1969, p. 77.

Chronology

1914   Julio Florencio Cortázar is born in Brussels, Belgium on 26 August. His father works for the Argentine foreign service.

1918   Family moves back to Argentina, to Banfield, a southern suburb of Buenos Aires, where "Los venenos" ("The Poison") and other stories take place.

1926   Cortázar begins studies at the Escuela Normal Mariano Acosta.

1935   Earns a degree as elementary school teacher from a teacher's college in Buenos Aires.

1937–1944   Teaches in secondary schools in the cities of Bolívar and Chivilcoy. Passes his first-year examinations at the university. Starts to write short stories.

1938   *Presencia*, a book of sonnets under the pseudonym of Julio Denis, is published by El Bibliófilo (Buenos Aires) in an author-sponsored edition.

1940   The prestigious literary magazine *Huella* publishes Cortázar's essay on Rimbaud.

1944–1945   Teaches courses in French literature at the University of Cuyo (subjects are Rimbaud and Mallarmé, but the syllabus also includes John Keats). Is active in the anti-Peronist movement and is arrested for political reasons and freed shortly thereafter. Essay on Keats is published. Jorge Luis Borges accepts and prints in *Los Anales de Buenos Aires* Cortázar's first major short story, "Casa tomada" ("House Taken Over").

1945–1951   Cortázar moves to Buenos Aires, where he works as manager of the Cámara Argentina del Libro. Reviews books (by Graham Greene, Octavio Paz, Cyril Connolly, etc.) and films (Luis Buñuel's *Los olvidados*, etc.) for Victoria Ocampo's magazine *Sur* and Francisco Ayala's *Realidad*.

Writes a collection of short stories, *La otra orilla* (The Other Shore), which would remain unpublished. Publishes an important study on John Keats's "Ode on a Grecian Urn." At the same time he earns a degree as a public translator and works for several Argentine publishing houses, translating works by André Gide, Walter de la Mare, G. K. Chesterton, Daniel Defoe, Marguerite Yourcenar, and Jean Giono, among others. Finishes a booklong essay on the contemporary novel, *Teoría del túnel* (Theory of the Tunnel), which would remain unpublished until 1994. Writes an obituary for Antonin Artaud and begins his obsession with surrealism. Refuses a chair at the University of Buenos Aires because of his opposition to the Juan Domingo Perón regime.

1949   *Los reyes* (The Kings) appears under the imprint Angel Gulab y Aldabahor (it is published under Cortázar's name in a limited edition by Daniel Devoto and the author). Reviews Leopoldo Marechal's *Adam Buenosayres*, and his text produces a small scandal. Writes the novel *El examen* (The Exam), which would be published posthumously.

1950   Publishes "Situación de la novela," an ambitious essay on modern trends in the novelistic genre.

1951   Is awarded a scholarship from the French government to study in Paris. Moves to France, where he will live until his death, dividing his time between Paris and the Provençal town of Saignon. The publication of the first collection of stories, *Bestiario* (Bestiary), by Editorial Sudamericana occurs the same month of his departure. Translates Louisa May Alcott's *Little Women*.

1952   Begins working for UNESCO as a translator.

1953   Marries Aurora Bernárdez, another Argentine translator. Visits Italy. Writes *Historias de cronopios y de famas*. Helped by Bernárdez, translates Edgar Allan Poe.

1956   *Final del juego* (*End of the Game*) appears under the imprint Los Presentes in Mexico, edited by Juan José Arreola. His translation of Poe's works (as *Obras en prosa*) appears.

1958   *Las armas secretas* (Secret Weapons) is published by Editorial Sudamericana.

1960 *Los premios* (*The Winners*), Cortázar's first published novel, appears. Visits the United States, mainly Washington, D.C., and New York.

1962 *Historias de cronopios y de famas* appears.

1963 *Rayuela* (*Hopscotch*), a masterful novel and his most durable work, is published to great acclaim. Critics immediately consider it a landmark of modern Latin American fiction. After identifying with Fidel Castro, visits Cuba for the first time.

1964 Second version of *Final del juego* appears in Buenos Aires, with 10 additional stories.

1966 *Todos los fuegos el fuego* (*All Fires the Fire*). Gregory Rabassa's English translation of *Rayuela* (as *Hopscotch*) appears in the United States. The Italian filmmaker Michelangelo Antonioni makes his movie *Blow-Up*, based on Cortázar's story "Las babas del diablo."

1967 *La vuelta al mundo en ochenta días* (*Around the Day in Eighty Worlds*). Travels to Greece; separates from Aurora Bernárdez.

1968 *62: Modelo para armar* (*62: A Model Kit*), a sequel of sorts to *Rayuela*, is published in Buenos Aires by Editorial Sudamericana.

1969 *Ultimo Round* (Last Round), what Cortázar calls "a collage book," appears in Mexico in two volumes.

1970 *Viaje alrededor de una mesa*. Visits Chile.

1971 *Pameos y Meopas*, his second collection of poems, appears.

1972 *Prosa del observatorio*, a volume of essays, is published.

1973 *El libro de Manuel* (*A Manual for Manuel*), his last novel and the most politically outspoken, appears. Travels to Argentina to promote the book. Visits Peru, Ecuador, and Chile.

1974 *Octaedro*. Participates in the PEN Translation Conference in New York.

1975 *Fantomas contra los vampiros multinacionales: Una utopía realizable narrada por Julio Cortázar*, a playful comic strip with political undertones, is published by Editorial Excélsior in Mexico. Lectures at the University of Oklahoma and in November dictates the Oklahoma Conference on Writers of the Hispanic World. Writes an introduction to Felisberto Hernández's *La casa inundada*. Attends session of the International Commission to Investigate the Crimes of the military junta in Chile.

1976 Visits Cuba and Nicaragua.

1977 *Alguien que anda por ahí* (Someone Walking Around) is published in Buenos Aires.

1978 *Territorios* (Territories) appears.

1979 *Un tal Lucas* (*A Certain Lucas*), a novel, is published. Becomes involved in the Russell Tribunal investigating crimes against people in Latin America.

1981 *Queremos tanto a Glenda* (We Love Glenda So Much). Accepts President François Mitterrand's offer of French citizenship while insisting he is not relinquishing his Argentine nationality.

1982 Carol Dunlop, Cortázar's companion during his last decade, dies in Paris.

1983 *Deshoras* (Bad Timing) appears in Mexico. A bit before, Cortázar and Dunlop collaborate on *Los autonautas en la cosmopista: o, Un viaje atemporal París-Marsella* (Autonauts of the Cosmopike; or, A Timeless Voyage Paris-Marseilles), with drawings by Stéphane Hérbert. With Argentine critic Ana María Barrenechea Cortázar publishes *Cuaderno de bitácora de "Rayuela"* (Hopscotch: Working Notebook). Visits Nicaragua and identifies with the Sandinistas. After a visit to Cuba, goes to New York to address the United Nations on the *desaparecidos* in South and Central America.

1984 *Nicaragua tan violentamente dulce* (Nicaraguan Sketches) and *Nada a Pehujó* (Nothing for Pahujó), a play in one act, are published in Barcelona and Mexico, respectively. Cortázar dies of leukemia and heart disease, probably AIDS-related, at Saint-Lazare Hospital in Paris, 12 February, and is buried in the Montparnasse cemetery. *Salvo el crepúsculo* (Except Dusk), poetic prose, appears.

1985   Plaza y Janés publishes in Spain Cortázar's *Textos políticos* (Political Writings).

1986   *El examen*, his second novel written (the first was burnt), is published by Editorial Sudamericana.

1994   Two-volume *Cuentos completos* (Complete Stories) and the three-volume *Obra crítica* (Critical Work) are published in Spain by Grupo Santillana's Editorial Alfaguara. They contain a couple of until-then unpublished works: *La Otra orilla* and *Teoría del túnel*.

Selected Bibliography

Primary Works
Story Collections

La otra orilla. 1945. Barcelona: Alfaguara, 1994. Contains "El hijo del vampiro," "Las manos que crecen," "Llama el teléfono, Delia," "Profunda siesta de Remi," "Puzzle," "Retorno de la noche," "Bruja," "Mudanza," "Distante espejo," "Los limpiadores de estrellas," "Breve curso de oceanografía," and "Estación de la mano."

Bestiario. Buenos Aires: Editorial Sudamericana, 1951. Contains "Casa tomada," "Carta a una señorita en París," "Lejana," "Omnibus," "Cefalea," "Circe," "Las puertas del cielo," and "Bestiario."

Final del juego. Mexico: Los Presentes, 1956; expanded edition, Buenos Aires: Editorial Sudamericana, 1964. Contains "Continuidad de los parques," "No se culpe a nadie," "El río," "Los venenos," "La puerta condenada," "Las ménades," "El ídolo de las cícladas," "Una flor amarilla," "Sobremesa," "La banda," "Los amigos," "El móvil," "Torito," "Relato con un fondo de agua," "Después del almuerzo," "Axolotl," "La noche boca arriba," and "Final del juego."

Las Armas secretas. Buenos Aires: Editorial Sudamericana, 1958. Contains "Cartas a mamá," "Los buenos servicios," "Las babas del diablo," "El perseguidor," and "Las armas secretas."

Todos los fuegos el fuego. Buenos Aires: Editorial Sudamericana, 1966. Contains "La autopista del sur," "La salud de los enfermos," "Reunión," "La Señorita Cora," "La isla a mediodía," "Instrucciones para John Howell," "Todos los fuegos el fuego," and "El otro cielo."

Ceremonias. Barcelona: Seix Barral, 1968. Consists of *Las armas secretas* and *Final del juego*.

Casa tomada. Graphic design by Juan Fresán. Buenos Aires: Editorial Minotauro, 1969. Reprint of the story included in *Bestiario*.

Relatos. Buenos Aires: Editorial Sudamericana, 1970. Consists of the stories of *Bestiario*, *Final del juego*, *Las armas secretas*, and *Todos los fuegos el fuego*, rearrenged under the headings "Rites," "Games," and "Passages."

La isla a mediodía y otros relatos. Barcelona: Salvat Editores, 1971. Contains 12 of Cortázar's best-known stories.

Octaedro. Buenos Aires: Editorial Sudamericana, 1974. Contains "Liliana llora-

148

ndo," "Los pasos en las huellas," "Manuscrito hallado en un bolsillo,"
"Verano," "Ahí pero dónde, cómo," "Lugar llamado Kindberg," "Las
fases de Severo," and "Cuello de gatito negro."

Antología. Introduction by Nicolás Bratosevich. Buenos Aires: La Librería,
1975.

Fantomas contra: Los vampiros multinacionales: Una utopía realizable. Mexico:
Exélsior, 1975.

Alguien que anda por ahí. Madrid: Alfaguara, 1977. Contains "Cambio de luces,"
"Vientos alisios," "Segunda vez," "Usted se tendió a tu lado," "En
nombre de Boby," "Apocalípsis en Solentiname," "La barca, o nueva
visita a Venecia," "Reunión con un círculo rojo," "Las caras de la med-
alla," "Alguien que anda por ahí," and "La noche de mantequilla."

Queremos tanto a Glenda. Madrid: Alfaguara, 1981. Contains "Orientación de
los gatos," "Queremos tanto a Glenda," "Historia con migalas," "Texto
en una libreta," "Recortes de prensa," "Tango de vuelta," "Clone,"
"Grafitti," "Historia que me cuento," and "Anillo de Moebius."

Deshoras. Mexico: Nueva Imagen, 1983. Contains "Botella de mar," "Fin de
etapa," "Segundo viaje," "Satarsa," "La escuela de noche," "Deshoras,"
"Pesadillas," and "Diario para un cuento."

Cuentos completos. 2 vols. Prologue by Mario Vargas Llosa. Barcelona: Alfaguara,
1994. Includes *La otra orilla, Historias de cronopios y de famas, Ultimo round,*
and *Un tal Lucas,* as well as all other stories published during his lifetime.

Story Collections in English

End of the Game and Other Stories. Translated by Paul Blackburn. New York:
Pantheon, 1963. Reprinted by Vintage in 1967 as *Blow-Up and Other Stories.*
Contains "Axolotl," "House Taken Over," "The Distances," "The Idol
of the Cyclades," "Letter to a Young Lady in Paris," "A Yellow Flower,"
"Continuity of Parks," "The Night Face Up," "Bestiary," "The Gates
of Heaven," "Blow-Up," "End of Game," "At Your Service," "The
Pursuer," and "Secret Weapons."

All Fires the Fire and Other Stories. Translated by Suzanne Jill Levine. New
York: Pantheon, 1973. Contains "Southern Thruway," "The Health of
the Sick," "Reunion," "Señorita Cora," "The Island at Noon," "Instructions for John Howell," "All Fires the Fire," and "The Other Heaven."

A Change of Light and Other Stories. Translated by Gregory Rabassa. New York:
Knopf, 1980. Contains "Summer," "In the Name of Bobby," "Liliana
Weeping," "A Place Named Kindberg," "Second Time Around," "Sev-
ero's Phases," "Butterball's Night," "Trade Winds," "MS Found in a
Pocket," "Apocalypse in Solentiname," "Footsteps in the Footprints,"
"Encounter within a Red Circle," "The Faces of the Medal," "Someone
Walking Around," "The Ferry; or, Another Trip to Venice," "There but
Where, How," "A Change of Light," and "Throat of a Black Kitten."

149

Selected Bibliography

We Love Glenda So Much and Other Tales. Translated by Gregory Rabassa. New York: Knopf, 1983. Contains "Orientation of Cats," "We Love Glenda So Much," "Story with Spiders," "Graffiti," "Clone," "Return Trip Tango," "Press Clippings," "Text in a Notebook," "Stories I Tell Myself," and "Moebius Strip."

Novels

Los reyes. [Dramatic Text.] Buenos Aires: Angel Gulab y Albadahor, 1949.
Los premios. Buenos Aires: Editorial Sudamericana, 1960.
Rayuela. Buenos Aires: Editorial Sudamericana, 1963.
62: Modelo para armar. Buenos Aires: Editorial Sudamericana, 1968.
El libro de Manuel. Buenos Aires: Editorial Sudamericana, 1972.
Un tal Lucas. Madrid: Alfaguara, 1979.
El examen. [1950]. Buenos Aires: Editorial Sudamericana, 1986.

Novels in English

The Winners. Translated by Elaine Kerrigan. New York: Pantheon, 1965.
Hopscotch. Translated by Gregory Rabassa. New York: Pantheon, 1966.
62: A Model Kit. Translated by Gregory Rabassa. New York: Pantheon, 1972.
A Manual for Manuel. Translated by Gregory Rabassa. New York: Pantheon, 1978.
A Certian Lucas. Translated by Gregory Rabassa. New York: Knopf, 1984.

Essays

Teoría del túnel. 1947. Introduction by Saúl Yurkievich. Barcelona: Alfaguara, 1994.
Historias de cronopios y de famas. Buenos Aires: Minotauro, 1962.
La vuelta al día en ochenta mundos. Mexico: Siglo XXI, 1967.
Cortázar lee a Cortázar. Buenos Aires: Laberinto, 1967.
Buenos Aires, Buenos Aires. Texts by Julio Cortázar. Photographs by Sara Facio and Alicia D'Amico. Buenos Aires: Editorial Sudamericana, 1968.
Ultimo round. Mexico: Siglo XXI, 1969.
Viaje alrededor de la mesa. Buenos Aires: Cuadernos de Rayuela, 1970.
Literatura en la revolución y revolución en la literatura: Oscar Collazos, Julio Cortázar, and Mario Vargas Llosa. Mexico: Siglo XXI, 1970.
Prosa del observatorio. Barcelona: Lumen, 1972.
Convergencias, divergencias, incidencias. Edited by Julio Ortega. Barcelona: Tusquets, 1973.
La casilla de los Morelli. Edited with a prologue and notes by Julio Ortega. Barcelona: Tusquets, 1973.

Selected Bibliography

Silvalandia. Texts by Julio Cortázar. Drawings by Julio Silva. Mexico: Ediciones Culturales G.D.A., 1975.

Territorios. Mexico: Siglo XXI, 1978.

Los autonautas de la cosmopista: o, un Viaje atemporal París-Marsella. Drawings by Stéphane Hérbert. Barcelona: Muchnick Editores, 1983.

Nicaragua tan violentamente dulce. Barcelona: Muchnick Editores, 1984.

Argentina: Años de alambradas culturales. Selected with notes by Saúl Yurkievich. Barcelona: Muchnick Editores, 1984.

Alto al Perú. Texts by Julio Cortázar. Photographs by Maruja Offerhaus. Mexico: Nueva Imagen, 1984.

Textos políticos. Barcelona: Plaza y Janés, 1985.

Obra crítica. 3 vols. Introductions by Saúl Yurkievich, Jaime Alazraki, and Saúl Sosnowski. Barcelona: Alfaguara, 1994.

Essays in English

Around the Day in Eighty Worlds. Translated by Thomas Christensen. San Francisco: North Point Press, 1986.

Cronopios and Famas. Translated by Paul Blackburn. New York: Pantheon, 1969.

Nicaraguan Sketches. Translated by Kathleen Weaver. New York: W. W. Norton, 1989.

Poetry

Presencia. [Pseud. Julio Denis.] Buenos Aires: El Bibliófilo, 1940.

Pameos y meopas. Barcelona: Libres de Sinera, 1971.

Salvo el crepúsculo. Mexico: Nueva Imagen, 1984.

Translations

Alcott, Louisa May. *Mujercitas.* Buenos Aires: Argos, 1951.

Brémond, Henry. *La poesía pura.* Buenos Aires: Rugos, 1947.

Chesterton, G. K. *El hombre que sabía demasiado.* Buenos Aires: Nova, n.d.

Defoe, Daniel. *Vida y extrañas y sorprendentes aventuras de Robinson Crusoe.* Buenos Aires: Viau, 1945.

Gide, André. *El inmoralista.* Buenos Aires: Argos, 1947.

Giono, Jean. *Nacimiento de la odisea.* Buenos Aires: Argos, 1946.

Lord Houghton. *Vida y cartas de John Keats.* Buenos Aires: Imán, 1955.

Poe, Edgar Allan. *Obras en prosa.* Vols. 1 and 2. San Juan, Puerto Rico: Ediciones de la Universidad de Puerto Rico and Revista de Occidente, 1956.

————. *Cuentos.* Havana: Editorial Nacional de Cuba, 1963.

————. *Aventuras de Arthur Gordon Pym.* Havana: Instituto del Libro, 1968.

Stern, Alfred. *Filosofía de la risa y del llanto.* Buenos Aires: Imán, 1950.

151

Selected Bibliography

————. *La filosofía existencial de Jean-Paul Sartre.* Buenos Aires: Imán, 1951.
Yourcenar, Marguerite. *Memorias de Adriano.* Buenos Aires: Sudamericana, 1955.

Secondary Works

Interviews

González Bermejo, Ernesto. *Conversaciones con Cortázar.* Barcelona: Edhasa, 1978.
Guibert, Rita. *Seven Voices: Seven Latin American Writers Talk to Rita Guibert,* 277–302. New York: Knopf, 1973.
Harss, Luis. *Into the Mainstream: Conversations with Latin American Writers,* 206–45. New York: Harper & Row, 1967.
Hernández, Ana María. "Conversación con Julio Cortázar." *Nueva Narrativa Hispanoamericana* 3, no. 2 (September 1973): 31–40.
Lartigue, Pierre. "Contar y cantar: Entrevista a Julio Cortázar y Saúl Yurkiévich." *Vuelta* 2, no. 17 (April 1978): 46–51.
Lebedev, Jorge. "Entrevista a Julio Cortázar." *Plural* 74 (1977): 31–37.
Picon Garfield, Evelyn. *Cortázar por Cortázar.* Veracruz, Mexico: Centro de Investigaciones Lingüístico-Literarias, Universidad Veracruzana, 1978.
Poniatowska, Elena. "La vuelta a Julio Cortázar en (cerca de) 80 preguntas." *Plural,* 6 May 1975, 28–36.
Prego, Omar. *La fascinación de las palabras: Conversaciones con Julio Cortázar.* Barcelona: Muchnik Editores, 1985.
Schneider, Luis Mario. "Julio Cortázar." *Revista de la Universidad de México* 17, no. 9 (May 1963): 24–25.
Soler Serrano, Joaquín. *Escritores a fondo.* Barcelona: Planeta, 1986: 71–86.
Sosnowski, Saúl. "Julio Cortázar." *Hispamérica* 5, no. 13 (April 1976): 51–68.
————. "Julio Cortázar: Modelos para desarmar." In *Espejo de escritores,* 39–62. Notes and Prologue by Reina Roffé. Hanover, N.H.: Ediciones del Norte, 1985.
Vargas Llosa, Mario. "Preguntas a Julio Cortázar." *Expreso* [Lima], 7 February 1965. Included in *Cinco miradas a Julio Cortázar,* edited by Ana María Simo, 83–91. Buenos Aires: Editorial Tiempo Contemporáneo, 1968.
————. "Entrevista a Julio Cortázar." *Comentarios bibliográficos americanos* 3, no. 11 (January–March 1971): 17–19.

Bibliographies

Becco, Jorge Horacio, and David William Foster. "Cortázar, Julio." In *La nueva narrativa hispanoamericana,* 78–100. Buenos Aires: Casa Pardo S.A., 1976.

Selected Bibliography

Flores, Angel, and Helene M. Anderson. "Cortázar, Julio." In *Masterpieces of Spanish American Literature*. Vol. 2, *Modernism to the Present*, 421–25. New York: Macmillan, 1974.

Paley de Francescato, Martha. "Bibliografía de y sobre Julio Cortázar." In *Revista Iberoamericana* 39, nos. 84–85 (July–December 1973): 697–726.

Yurkiévich, Gladis. "Bibliografía [de y sobre J.C.]." In Ernesto González Bermejo, *Conversaciones con Cortázar*, 149–90. Barcelona: EDHASA, 1978.

Criticism

Alazraki, Jaime. *En busca del unicornio: Los cuentos de Julio Cortázar: Elementos para una poética de lo neofantástico*. Madrid: Gredos, 1983.

———. "Los últimos cuentos de Julio Cortázar." *Revista Iberoamericana* 51, nos. 130–31 (January–June 1985): 21–41.

Alazraki, Jaime, and Ivar Ivask, eds. *The Final Island: The Fiction of Julio Cortázar*. Norman: University of Oklahoma Press, 1978.

Arriguci, Davi, Jr. *O Escorpiao encalacrado: A poética da destruicao em Julio Cortázar*. Sao Paulo: Perspectiva, 1973.

Bennett, Maurice. "A Dialogue of Gazes: Metamorphosis and Epiphany in Julio Cortázar's 'Axolotl.' " *Studies in Short Fiction* 23 (Winter 1986): 57–61.

Campa, Rosalba. *La Realtá e il suo anagrama: Il modello narrativo nei recconti di Julio Cortázar*. Pisa, Italy: Giardini, 1978.

Curuchet, Juan Carlos. *Julio Cortázar o la crítica de la razón pragmática*. Madrid: Editora Nacional, 1972. Domínguez, Mignón. *Cartas desconocidas de Julio Cortázar: 1939–1945*. Buenos Aires: Editorial Sudamericana, 1992.

Ferré, Rosario. *Cortázar: El Romántico en su observatorio*. Puerto Rico: Editorial Cultural, 1990.

Filer, Malva. *Los Mundos de Julio Cortázar*. New York: Las Américas, 1970.

Giacomán, Helmy F., ed. *Homejane a Julio Cortázar*. New York: Las Américas-Anaya, 1972.

González Bermejo, Ernesto. *Cosas de escritores: Gabriel García Márquez, Mario Vargas Llosa y Julio Cortázar*. Montevideo: Biblioteca de Marcha, 1971.

Hernández del Castillo, Ana María. *Keats, Poe, and Cortázar's Mythopoesis*. Amsterdam: John Benjamin, 1981.

Lagmanovich, David, ed. *Estudios sobre los cuentos de Julio Cortázar*. Barcelona: Hispamérica, 1975.

Lastra, Pedro, ed. *El escritor y la crítica: Julio Cortázar*. Madrid: Taurus, 1981.

MacAdam, Alfred. *El individuo y el otro: Crítica de los cuentos de Julio Cortázar*. Buenos Aires: La Librería, 1971.

Martínez Cruzado, América. *The Philosophical and Mystic Aspects of Poe, Baudelaire, and Cortázar*. Champaign: University of Illinois Press, 1976.

Mastrangelo, Carlos. *Usted, yo, los cuentos de Julio Cortázar y su autor*. Córdoba: Universidad Nacional de Córdoba, 1971.

Mora Valcárcel, Carmen de. *Teoría y práctica del cuento en los relatos de Julio*

Selected Bibliography

Cortázar. Seville: Publicaciones de la Escuela de Altos estudios de Sevilla, 1982.

Panells, Antonio. *Cortázar: Metafísica y erotismo*. Madrid: José Porrúa Turanzas S.A., 1979.

Parkinson, Lois. "Movement and Stasis, Film and Photo: Temporal Structures in the Recent Fiction of Julio Cortázar." *Review of Contemporary Fiction 3*, no. 3 (Fall 1983): 51–65.

Paz, Octavio. "Laude (Julio Cortázar, 1914–1984)." In *Al paso*. Barcelona: Seix Barral, 1992.

Peavler, Terry J. *Julio Cortázar*. New York: Twayne Publishers, 1990.

Pérez, Genaro J. "Auto-referential Elements in 'Blow-Up' and 'The Gates of Heaven.' " *Review of Contemporary Fiction 3*, no. 3 (Fall 1983): 48–51.

Picon Garfield, Evelyn. *¿Es Julio Cortázar un surrealista?* Madrid: Gredos, 1975.

———. *Julio Cortázar*. New York: Frederick Ungar Publishing, 1975.

Rein, Mercedes. *Julio Cortázar: El escritor y sus máscaras*. Montevideo: Diaco, 1969.

Roy, Joaquín. *Julio Cortázar ante su sociedad*. Barcelona: Península, 1974.

Scholz, László. *El arte poética de Julio Cortázar*. Buenos Aires: Castaóeda, 1977.

Simo, Ana María, ed. *Cinco miradas sobre Cortázar*. Buenos Aires: Editorial Tiempo Conteporáneo, 1968.

Sola, Graciela de. *Julio Cortázar y el hombre nuevo*. Buenos Aires: Editorial Sudamericana, 1968.

Sosnowski, Saul. *Julio Cortázar: Una búsqueda mítica*. Buenos Aires: Noé, 1973.

Stavans, Ilan. "Julio Cortázar, 'La puerta condenada,' y los fantasmas," *Plural* [Mexico] 17–18, no. 204 (1988): 86–90.

———. "Kafka, Cortázar, Gass." *Review of Contemporary Fiction 11*, no. 3 (1991): 131–36.

———. "¿Un Julio Cortázar enpolvado?" *Epoca* [Mexico] 21 (31 July 1994): 34–35.

Vargas Llosa, Mario. "La trompeta de Deýa." *Vuelta* 195 (February 1993): 10–14.

Vinocur, Sara, and Néstor Tirri, eds. *La vuelta a Cortázar en nueve ensayos*. Buenos Aires: Carlos Pérez, 1968.

Yovanovich, Gordana. *Julio Cortázar's Character Mosaic*. Toronto, Buffalo, and London: University of Toronto Press, 1990.

Special Journal Issues Devoted to Cortázar

Boletín de Literaturas Hispánicas [Santa Fé, Argentina], Facultad de Filosofía y Letras, Instituto de Letras, Universidad Nacional de Litoral, number 6, 1966.

Books Abroad [Norman, Oklahoma] 50, no. 3 (Summer 1976).

Casa de las Américas [Havana, Cuba] 25, nos. 145–46 (July–October 1984).

Selected Bibliography

Cuadernos Hispanoamericanos [Madrid], nos. 364–66 (October–December 1980).
Review [New York] 72, no. 7 (winter 1972).
Review of Contemporary Fiction 3, no. 3 (Fall 1983).
Revista Iberoamericana [University of Pittsburgh] 39, nos. 84–85 (July–December 1973).

Index

Index

Index

Index

The Author

Ilan Stavans, a novelist and critic, teaches at Amherst College. His Spanish-language works include *Talia y el cielo* (1979; rev. 1989), which won the 1992 Latino Literature Prize; the story collection *La pianista manca* (1992), awarded the Gramma Literature Prize in Spain; *Antiheroes: México y su novela policial* (1993); and the essay collections *Prontuario* (1991) and *La pluma y la máscara* (1993). In English he has written *Imagining Columbus: The Literary Voyage* (1993), winner of the 1993 Bernard M. Baruch Excellence in Scholarship Award; *The Hispanic Condition: Reflections on Culture and Identity in America*, (1995); and *Bandido: Oscar "Zeta" Acosta and the Chicano Experience* (1995). He has translated Felipe Alfau into English in a bilingual edition of *Sentimental Songs* (1992) and edited (with Harold Augenbraum) *Growing Up Latino: Memoirs and Stories* (1993), as well as *Tropical Synagogues: Short Stories by Jewish–Latin American Writers* (1994). He has been nominated for the National Book Critics Circle Award for Excellence in Book Reviewing.

The Editor

General Editor Gordon Weaver earned his B.A. in English at the University of Wisconsin-Milwaukee in 1961; his M.A. in English at the University of Illinois, where he studied as a Woodrow Wilson Fellow, in 1962; and his Ph.D. in English and creative writing at the University of Denver in 1970. His novels include *Count a Lonely Cadence*, *Give Him a Stone*, *Circling Byzantium*, and *The Eight Corners of the World*. Many of his short stories are collected in *The Entombed Man of Thule*, *Such Waltzing Was Not Easy*, *Getting Serious*, *Morality Play*, *A World Quite Round*, and *Men Who Would Be Good*. He edited *The American Short Story, 1945–1980: A Critical History*, and is currently editor of *Cimarron Review*. He is professor of English at Oklahoma State University and serves as an adjunct member of the faculty of the Vermont College Master of Fine Arts in Writing Program.